INTERNATIONAL SECURITY

D0869034

The Royal Institute of International Affairs is an unofficial body which promotes the scientific study of international questions and does not express opinions of its own. The opinions expressed in this publication are the responsibility of the author.

The Institute gratefully acknowledges the comments and suggestions of the following who read the manuscript on behalf of the Research Committee: Dr Wolf Mendl, Dr Roger Morgan, and Michael Howard.

INTERNATIONAL SECURITY

Reflections on Survival and Stability

Edited by

Kenneth J. Twitchett

Issued under the auspices of the
Royal Institute of International Affairs

OXFORD UNIVERSITY PRESS

LONDON   OXFORD   NEW YORK

1971

Oxford University Press

LONDON OXFORD NEW YORK

GLASGOW TORONTO MELBOURNE WELLINGTON

CAPE TOWN SALISBURY IBADAN NAIROBI DAR ES SALAAM LUSAKA

ADDIS ABABA BOMBAY CALCUTTA MADRAS KARACHI LAHORE DACCA

KUALA LUMPUR SINGAPORE HONG KONG TOKYO

SBN 19 285048 2

First published as an Oxford University Press
paperback by Oxford University Press, London, 1971

Printed in Great Britain by
The Eastern Press, Limited, London and Reading

CONTENTS

ABBREVIATIONS

NOT EXPLAINED IN THE TEXT

CENTO   Central Treaty Organization

COMECON   Council for Mutual Economic Assistance

EEC   European Economic Community

EFTA   European Free Trade Association

FAO   Food and Agriculture Organization

ISS   Institute for Strategic Studies

NATO   North Atlantic Treaty Organization

OECD   Organization for Economic Co-operation and Development

SEATO   South-East Asia Collective Defence Treaty Organization

UNCTAD   UN Conference on Trade and Development

WEU   Western European Union

PREFACE

THE four chapters of this book are designed to offer an introduction to some of the considerations involved in contemporary problems of international security. In the first chapter I attempt to probe the meaning and the various implications of the concept of security itself, and to analyse some of the methods whereby states can endeavour to safeguard their external security in combination and/or through collaboration with other states. The other three chapters are more specific and deal with concrete issues of current policy. Neville Brown examines the intricate and agonizing security problems posed by technological developments in the realm of weapons of mass destruction and by wider factors of a social and economic nature such as population pressures and competition for natural resources, which might lead to collective violence. Alan James analyses the record and the likely future of the United Nations as an instrument for furthering international security, including the employment of UN peace-keeping forces. Finally, Peter Nailor unravels the history of the European aspect of the cold war and the prospects for a meaningful solution to the problems of European security. At the end of each chapter there is a short guide to further reading.

All four chapters are based on historical-political approaches, not behaviourist or scientific ones. It should also be noted that throughout the book, unless otherwise indicated, the focus is on external military security rather than on the means whereby states seek to strengthen their internal security or the economic and other aspects of security. While the book comprises an integral whole, each chapter consists of a self-contained essay which probes differing aspects of contemporary security problems. The complex and interrelated ramifications of these problems, however, result in some unavoidable overlapping between the four chapters.

Although the security problems confronting China and the members of the so-called third world are examined, the book as a whole is essentially Eurocentric, focusing as it does on security problems involving the two super-powers and the states of Europe. This Eurocentricity reflects not only limitations of space, but also the fact that security in Europe has been the subject of fairly detailed proposals and discussions involving the replacement of the existing system of military alliances by a European-wide security system with its own institutional framework. Similar suggestions have been made for other areas, but within them some existing conflicts are perhaps too bitter and the consensus necessary for region-wide security systems is probably unlikely to develop in the foreseeable future. Indeed, it is extremely doubtful whether such a system can easily be established in Europe, let alone in, say, the Middle East or South-east Asia. Even if such systems were to develop in the third world, both the Soviet Union and the United States, and possibly the traditional great powers of Western Europe, could almost certainly not avoid being either guarantors of and/or participants in them. For these states, the main priority remains the safeguarding of military security in Europe. Moreover, these states are the most important 'actors'[1] in wider global problems of security involving the control of weapons of mass destruction, concerted international attacks on world poverty, and the employment of UN peace-keeping techniques, and they will probably remain so for a long time to come. Eurocentricity results neither from European arrogance nor from the authors' collective myopia, but rather from a realistic appreciation of the international facts of life.

None of the four chapters either purports to provide blueprints for future security or to present overall conclusions. Our collective views are somewhat pessimistic. It is to be hoped that the picture we paint is not too black. But that is for the reader and the future to judge.

Aberdeen,
August 1970

K. J. T.

[1] The sense is that used in Carol Ann Cosgrove & K. J. Twitchett, *The New International Actors: the UN and the EEC* (1970).

ACKNOWLEDGEMENTS

THE contributions to this book by Neville Brown, Alan James, and Peter Nailor are based on papers delivered to the International Relations section of the Twentieth Annual Conference of the Political Studies Association of the United Kingdom, held at Christchurch College, Oxford, April 1970. All four contributors wish to express their gratitude to the PSA and to the participants in the conference for their useful criticisms. Special debts of gratitude are owed to Miss Hermia Oliver and Dr Roger Morgan of Chatham House for their invaluable criticisms, ideas, and general assistance in compiling this book. The responsibility for any inaccuracies or misinterpretations belong to the four contributors alone.

1

STRATEGIES FOR SECURITY:
SOME THEORETICAL CONSIDERATIONS

Kenneth J. Twitchett

IT is widely accepted that the security of a state is of vital importance. But what is security? The existence of a real problem of definition is indicated by the large body of literature attempting to explain what is involved in safeguarding international security. Most of the concepts and terms used are at best no more than intelligent assumptions and generalizations based on what seem to be the interests and actions of most states for most of the time. They cannot be more than this because of the conditional nature of the large range of imponderables and unique variables involved in specific questions of international security. The views of particular individuals on what constitutes international security are themselves subjective and inclined to fluctuate in respect of the values they emphasize. The problem of definition is even more complicated now than it was in former times. Traditionally, military security was almost always the primary concern of both statesmen and commentators, but in the modern world economic considerations and welfare values are of increasing importance.[1]

For these reasons the first part of this chapter attempts to clarify some of the considerations implicit in national security in the external sense. Because security is related to and dependent on them, there is also a brief examination of the concepts of national interests, ' objective ', power, and force. The second part of the chapter analyses some strategies by which

---

[1] All students of international relations are, of course, confronted by problems of relativity, subjectivity, and the unique variables involved in particular international questions. For a fuller examination, see K. J. Twitchett, ' Some Problems Confronting Students of International Relations ', *Political Studies*, Sept. 1969, pp. 357–64.

states try to safeguard their security in the diplomatic milieu. There is some investigation of unilateral strategies, but the primary emphasis is on three models whereby a state can search for security in combination with and/or through collaboration with other states: namely, balance of power, collective security, and contemporary collective defence and regional arrangements. The term ' collaboration ' is used to denote strategies for security which promise future assistance, usually but not always mutual and military in character. Throughout the primary focus is on external military rather than on economic security or on the means whereby states endeavour to strengthen the often delicate fabric of their own internal security. But implicit in much of the argument is the supposition that in some respects economic considerations are now more important than military ones.

I. The External Security of States

The word ' security ' itself is not easy to define. The problems involved are not altogether semantic in origin. Dictionary definitions usually refer to ' freedom from danger, fear, or attack '—words which themselves are not synonymous. In all three senses security is subjective and relative to the internal and external environment of particular human societies. Possibly the only common denominator is that absolute security is an unrealizable goal. In the context of actual or theoretical international systems in which states are the principal actors, the search for freedom from danger, fear, or attack is frequently a self-defeating objective. The additional security obtained by one state can result in a feeling of insecurity by other states, who in turn might well seek to increase their margin of security by means which the first state sees as a threat. The end-product is frequently a vicious circle in relative if not in absolute terms. This is especially true if the states in question define their security in military terms, but also occurs if it is defined in economic or other terms.

Despite the inherent pitfalls, many commentators have courageously attempted to define what is implied by the external security of states. For example, Professor Frederick H. Hartman argues that ' security is the sum total of the vital national interests of the state '. He amplifies this by stating that ' a vital national interest is one for which a [state] is willing to go to war either immediately or ultimately '. Consequently, ' concepts of national security will vary from state to state in proportion to the concept of vital national interests that any given state entertains at any given time '. [2]

Although a useful starting point, this definition is contentious, especially as it depends on notions of national interest. This term is helpful in indicating policy demands made by the state rather than those of private individuals, pressure groups, sub-national groupings, or humanity as a whole. But as Arnold Wolfers warns, political formulas such as ' national interest ' should be scrutinized with particular care once they achieve popular appeal. ' They may not mean the same thing to different people ', and indeed ' may not have any precise meaning at all '. They may therefore permit ' everyone to label whatever policy he favours with an attractive and possibly deceptive name '. [3] He draws attention to a striking change of emphasis in American perceptions of national interests. At the height of the cold war especially, most Americans perceived these in terms of an ability to resist Soviet military aggression and ideological subversion, but in the middle of the 1930s the emphasis was usually placed on domestic-economic and welfare considerations. [4]

K. J. Holsti attempts to avoid the ambiguities associated with national interest by replacing it with ' the concept of objective ', which he understands as implying ' essentially an *image* of a future state of affairs and future set of conditions which governments through individual policy-makers aspire to bring about by wielding influence abroad and by changing or sustaining the behaviour of other states '. [5] Although providing a useful analytical tool which avoids the emotive prescriptions for action often associated with national interest,

---

[2] See *The Relations of Nations* (New York, 1967), p. 14.

[3] *Discord and Collaboration* (Baltimore, 1962), p. 147. The ideas and theoretical considerations on security set forth in the first part of this chapter owe a considerable intellectual debt to Professor Wolfers. I have adapted them and the responsibility for any misconceptions, etc., are, of course, mine alone.

[4] Ibid., pp. 147-8.

[5] See his *International Politics* (Englewood Cliffs, 1967), p. 126.

the concept is vague and open-ended. It embraces a multitude of foreign-policy interests ranging from primary goals directly determining the very survival of the state to such relatively minor ones as the passing of a favourable resolution in the UN General Assembly. Furthermore, policy-makers themselves do not usually base their actions on carefully formulated logical and coherent sets of objectives. Most governmental transactions are routine or unplanned, and important decisions often made in response to the urgent pressures of particular crises rather than as part of a coherent and far-sighted policy. It is also necessary to distinguish between the ' declaratory ' and the ' operational ' objectives of policy-makers. This is especially important when they are trying to promote such intangible values as the achievement of international prestige. Professor Holsti himself points out that ' some objectives remain constant over centuries and directly involve the lives and welfare of all members of a national society. Others change almost daily and concern only a handful of governmental personnel and citizens '.[6]

He endeavours to overcome these problems by dividing objectives into three categories, based on the degrees of commitment to achieve specific objectives, the time element for their realization, and on the demands placed on other states. The three categories are (1) ' core values and interests ', (2) ' middle-range goals which normally impose demands on other states ', and (3) ' universal long-range goals, which seldom have definite time limits '.[7] It is clearly the preservation of ' core values ' which have to be regarded as vitally important to the security of a state, especially where this affects its very survival. As Walter Lippmann has maintained, a state ' is secure to the extent to which it is not in danger of having to sacrifice core values if it wishes to avoid war, and is able, if challenged, to maintain them by victory in such a war '.[8] This definition must in turn be amplified, especially as regards the relationship of security with ' power ' and ' core values '.

[6] Ibid., pp. 126–7.

[7] Ibid., pp. 131–2.

[8] *US Foreign Policy: Shield of the Republic* (Boston, 1943), p. 51 (quoted in *Discord & Collaboration*, p. 150).

The Lippmann definition accords with the usual understanding of security being a function of a state's ability to deter, and if necessary defeat, an attack. This in turn depends on a state's power. Although sometimes regarded as such, power and security are not synonymous. Power is a relative concept representing the means whereby such values as security are safeguarded. Many commentators would agree with Inis Claude's use of power to denote ' essentially military capability —the elements which contribute directly or indirectly to the capacity to coerce, kill, and destroy '.[9] Force is usually understood as the actual exercise of such power. The use of the word ' capacity ' is unfortunate since a state might possess the capacity but not the ability to destroy another state in the course of armed hostilities. For example, the United States possesses the military capacity to obliterate North Vietnam in a few minutes, but is restrained from doing so both by her own moral scruples and by the fear of possible Soviet or Chinese retaliation. More significantly, the mutual nuclear capabilities of the United States and the Soviet Union provide a check on their abilities to employ them.

Professor Claude himself points out that ' power may be defined much more broadly, to include the variety of means by which states may pursue their purposes and affect the behaviour of other units '.[10] In fact, many contemporary international relationships depend more on economic, psychological, and even moral factors than military strength. In this wider sense power can be defined as the ability of a state to influence the actions of other international actors—usually states, but some international organizations and occasionally international business corporations come into this category.[11] Nevertheless, power in the military sense has historically been the most important means whereby states have attempted to ensure their security. Like their forebears, contemporary statesmen

[9] See Inis L. Claude, Jr., *Power and International Relations* (New York, 1962), p. 6.
[10] Ibid.
[11] For a fuller exposition of the point, see Carol Ann Cosgrove & K. J. Twitchett, *The New International Actors: the UN and the EEC* (London, 1970), and George Modelski, ' The Corporation in World Society ', *Year Book of World Affairs, 1968*, pp. 64–79.

are apt to equate peace with security and view both as a by-product of a favourable margin of power. Military weakness in relation to hostile or potentially hostile neighbours and peace by self-abnegation has never had much appeal. Most 'realists' would agree with Nicholas Spykman's contention that in the world of states 'the struggle for power is identical with the struggle for survival, and the improvement of the relative power position becomes the primary objective of the internal and the external policy of states '.[12] But the maxim that states endeavour to preserve their independence by acquiring a favourable margin of military power is by no means an 'iron law ' of international politics. Sparta may have been a military fortress, Athens at the peak of its grandeur was not. Even in the present day, when governments of industrialized states possess a much greater ability to harness the physical resources of their states than ever before, most if not all place a limit on the price they are willing to pay for military security. As Arnold Wolfers points out, 'every increment of security must be paid for by additional sacrifices of other values usually of a kind more exacting than the mere expenditure of precious time on the part of policy-makers '.[13]

Cost rather than moral scruple is probably the main reason why some states signed the Nuclear Non-Proliferation Treaty.[14] Although presenting their signatures as contributions to world disarmament, Britain and other Western European states could afford to make such moral gestures because of the shelter of the American nuclear umbrella. If that umbrella were withdrawn or failed to deter a full-scale Soviet attack on Western Europe as a whole or on specific states, their own military power, individually or collectively, would almost certainly not be sufficient to repulse such an attack or to ensure their survival. Many states do not possess such external guarantees of their security. Israel depends essentially on her

[12] Quoted in Harold & Margaret Sprout, *Foundations of International Politics* (Princeton, 1962), p. 115.

[13] *Discord & Collaboration*, p. 158.

[14] Whether the cost of nuclear weapons will remain prohibitive is, of course, another question. The possibilities of nuclear proliferation are discussed by Neville Brown in ch. 2.

own military will to withstand the constant Arab threats to her survival. But even she does not harness her total resources to fashion a more effective military machine—the cost in other values would be too high. Another consideration is that even expenditure on military power might not result in the desired degree of security. For instance, Czechoslovakia, although she possessed one of the best trained and equipped armies in Europe, at the time of the Munich Agreement of 1938, refrained from using force to resist German aggression. She possibly possessed the capacity to do so but not the will. An alternative situation may arise when the expenditure is on weapons unsuitable for achieving the required security objective: the vast American expenditure on thermonuclear weapons yields little return in attempts to subdue the Vietcong, since other, less costly, weapons are needed. More significantly, it is doubtful if their vast outlays on nuclear weapons would ensure the survival of either the United States or the Soviet Union as a viable political unit in the event of an unlimited nuclear war between them. At most their nuclear arsenals can only deter aggression; they might afford relative but not absolute security. In fact, the nuclear competition of the super-powers provokes mutual counter-measures which tend to lead to the vicious circle already mentioned, a dilemma which itself causes insecurity.

At the non-nuclear level the American intervention in the Dominican Republic in 1965 and the Soviet invasion of Czechoslovakia in 1968 demonstrate that both super-powers are still willing and able to take unilateral military action if they perceive threats to vital national interests within their respective clearly delineated spheres of influence. Nevertheless, in contemporary diplomatic circles generally, there is ' increased doubt as to the moral propriety of force . . . accompanied by growing awareness of the limitations upon its practical value '.[15] As Alan James has pointed out, the use of force, besides giving rise to immediate difficulties, may not be beneficial in the longer term because ' it cannot be relied upon to solve problems or to set in train a process which

[15] See Ditchley Foundation, *The Role of Force in International Order and United Nations Peace-Keeping* (1969), by Alan James (Rapporteur), p. 8.

will lead to their solution '. In fact, it ' contains within itself the seeds of its own expansion ' because either frustration or an initial success ' can present a powerful temptation to enlarge the level of one's intervention or extend one's objectives '. There is also the tendency of force ' to leave a legacy of bitterness or exhaustion ' which could provide a basis for a future threat to ' the newly established order of things '.[16]

Security can also depend on factors other than military power. One example, in modern times at least, is that the security of small states largely stems from the forbearance of their stronger neighbours rather than their own efforts. The part that treaty guarantees can play in safeguarding the security of small states is demonstrated by the respect of the European great powers for Belgium's neutrality and independence during the second half of the nineteenth century. Alternatively, security might depend on economic factors or diplomatic skill rather than military strength. But these will not be sufficient to ensure survival if there are no restraints on hostile or potentially hostile neighbours. Two successful neutrals, Sweden and Switzerland, have fashioned small but efficient armies, for not to do so could well have meant their extinction as independent states. Even so, claims that security depends solely or even primarily on military power should be treated with special caution.

Another important point is that there is no uniformity in the search by states for security—they are not constantly or similarly confronted with the same degree or type of danger. While no state can be absolutely safe from attack, it would be absurd to maintain that, say, Mexico is at present confronted by the same degree of danger as Thailand. Professor Wolfers has maintained that security is a core value which a state ' can have more or less and which it can aspire to have in greater or lesser measure '.[17] But even if there is agreement on the amount of security required, there might still be disagreement on the means for achieving it. This point is illustrated by the public debate during the late 1950s on whether Britain's security depended on acquiring a viable nuclear capability.

[16] Ibid., pp. 7–8.
[17] *Discord & Collaboration*, p. 150.

In this case, as with similar debates in other states, there was also considerable disagreement on whether Britain could in fact defend herself. Such disagreements stem principally from the inability of policy-makers accurately to forecast the future. They can never objectively measure the chance, source, and scale of future danger—these can only be matters of subjective evaluation and speculation, coloured by the predilections of particular observers. Some evaluations may be more accurate than others, but none can carry certain guarantees. In fact, like national interests, security core values are essentially relative and subjective. Much depends on the images perceived of core values and the importance attached to them by particular individuals, and by the same individuals at different times.

So far it has been implicitly assumed that the survival of the state is the primary core value. Is this assumption, in fact, valid? There is certainly much truth in Inis Claude's contention that ' peace at any price has never appealed to the bulk of mankind, even when peace seemed the indispensable condition of survival '[18] and in Hans Morgenthau's belief that ' the survival of a political unit, such as a [state] in its identity is the irreducible minimum, the necessary element of its interests *vis a vis* other units '.[19] Nevertheless, the survival of the state is by no means the only core value, or even always the most important one, perceived by political leaders and other opinion makers.

This qualification is especially pertinent to situations involving the possibility of nuclear conflict. Discussion of this question is, of course, largely a matter of conjecture as there are fortunately only theoretical case studies to draw upon, but some hypothetical observations can be made. The most important is that in such situations the views of Professors Claude and Morgenthau, just cited, could well be contradictory rather than complementary and parallel. This is not in line with the basic assumption of some contemporary theories of nuclear deterrence that neither super-power would back down if

---

[18] *Power & Internat. Relations*, p. 4.
[19] ' Another " Great Debate ": the National Interest of the United States ', *American Political Science Review*, xlvi (1952), pp. 971–8.

threatened with nuclear attack by the other. But would this actually occur if the crisis escalated to the point whereby a failure to back down would probably involve a full-scale nuclear attack on a super-power's metropolitan territory? The assumption may be doubted in view of the possible cost of some forty million dead, the tremendous destruction to property, and the chaos resulting from the breakdown of a sophisticated industrialized society. Of what real import is the consideration that the threatened super-power could also destroy its adversary? This would not bring about its own resurrection. Similar doubts are also permissible regarding nuclear threats to security interests not situated in the metropolitan territory of a super-power. Would President J. F. Kennedy have actually risked a nuclear holocaust if Premier Khrushchev had refused to order the dismantling of the Russian rocket bases in Cuba? Conversely, would Premier Khrushchev have dismantled them if the offending bases had been situated in, say, Poland not Cuba? In both cases, could the leaders of either the Soviet Union or the United States have been absolutely certain of their ability to prevent the crises escalating to the brink of total nuclear war?

Minor nuclear states like Britain and France, or non-nuclear ones, might well find capitulation preferable to possible annihilation if threatened with nuclear blackmail by a super-power. High population densities and lack of viable delivery systems severely restrict the British and French capabilities to pose real and meaningful counter nuclear threats. Their first-strike nuclear capabilities are not really credible and the effectiveness of their second-strike ones is doubtful to say the least. They would find it extremely difficult to resist such nuclear blackmail unless they had the wholehearted support of the other super-power. Would a super-power, in fact, offer support if this might result in a nuclear attack on its own metropolitan territory? Even if the support were proffered, would the assisted state then be willing to countenance the possible cost of its own nuclear devastation?

In all these hypothetical situations, statesmen would have the moral choice between national pride and state survival.

The choice would have to be made in conditions of great uncertainty and severe psychological strain. Would rational decision-making be feasible in such conditions? To choose national pride could jeopardize the very physical existence of the state. To choose state survival could well subject it to future blackmail. With either choice, the quality and the actual existence of human life would, it is to be hoped, be the paramount consideration. Fortunately, in the foreseeable future these choices might never have to be made as there is at present a real restraint on the two super-powers; neither can be completely certain of each other's intentions or actual nuclear capabilities. But the possibilities of accident, miscalculation, and even the advent of a ' mad Caesar ', cannot be wholly ruled out—highly unlikely developments, yes, but still possible.

It would certainly be a more dangerous world if either super-power achieved, or believed that it had achieved, unchallengeable nuclear supremacy. Alternatively, what would be the situation in the unlikely event of the Soviet Union and the United States employing their nuclear arsenals in concert? Communist China's future accession to the rank of nuclear super-power is yet another imponderable. A more dangerous world can also be postulated if there is widespread nuclear proliferation—the potentialities of chemical and microbiological weapons pose a further threat for the future. Such conflicts as the Arab-Israeli embroilment or a future Black African confrontation with South Africa could involve the use of, or the threat to use, weapons of mass destruction. Again, the population explosion might predispose the poor non-white peoples to acquire and to threaten to use such weapons in making demands on the rich, white peoples. Statesmen might even be confronted with the demands of non-governmental groups possessing these weapons. The current activities of aeroplane hi-jackers might well be a portent for the future. It is conceivable that state survival might come to depend on peace at any price!

The survival of the state has not always been the most important core value, even when weapons of mass destruction have not been involved. In fact, the existence of the state has been an obstacle to the ambitions of some political leaders, as in the 1930s when the leaders of the Austrian Nazi Party believed that the most important value to strive for was Austria's incorporation into the Third Reich rather than her survival as a sovereign state. The leaders of other national minorities have desired their peoples' incorporation within what they perceive as the national homeland—witness the efforts of the Somali minorities in Kenya and Ethiopia to join the Republic of Somalia. Other national minorities, like the Hungarian citizens of the Habsburg Empire in the nineteenth century, have placed the highest priority on forming their own independent state. A more contemporary example is afforded by the tragic efforts of the Biafrans to break away from Nigeria.

Other groups apart from dissatisfied national minorities believed and still believe that the survival of the state is by no means the highest core value. The pre-1917 Russian Bolsheviks professed a distaste for a world divided into sovereign states—their ideology emphasized class values, not the political divisions of statehood. The fervent advocates of world government or, say, European federalism, also come into this general category. They believe that the larger community would ensure higher levels of order, justice, and peace than is afforded by existing state structures.

Even if an alternative political structure appears to be an unattractive proposition, the survival of the state is not necessarily the highest core value. For example, the Czechoslovakian failure to resist the German and Russian invasions of 1938–9 and 1968 demonstrates that the country's leaders had a higher core value than its survival as an independent political unit. They presumably believed that the likely enormous cost to the Czechoslovakian people in terms of loss of life and destruction of property did not justify what would have probably been no more than futile attempts at military resistance. To them the most important core value was the welfare of the people rather than state survival as such.

In non-conflict situations, welfare values themselves are of increasing importance, to the detriment of ones emphasizing external military security. This is especially so in the industrialized democracies of the West. There is much truth in James Avery Joyce's contention that ' the spirit of *Pacem in Terris* is closer to the hearts and minds of ordinary people than NATO's balance of terror '.[20] Such values are seemingly not only held by many ordinary people, but have also influenced the actions of policy-makers. Britain, for example, under the Wilson government opted for the welfare state rather than a credible nuclear capacity or a meaningful strategic role east of Suez. The United States must also apparently choose between welfare needs, on the one hand, and unlimited expenditure on attempting to forge an impenetrable nuclear shield and an active global foreign policy, on the other. Even the leaders of the Soviet Union must now give the Russian people some ' butter ' as well as ' guns '. The third world is not immune from such values. The overthrow of Presidents Nkrumah and Sukarno are a warning to those African and Asian leaders tempted to concentrate on military security and/or an active foreign policy to the neglect of their people's economic welfare.

It is by no means claimed that welfare values are as yet the most important values, merely that they are assuming a growing importance. But if the technological revolution continues to accelerate, and if there is no nuclear holocaust, some observers postulate their predominance in what they term the future ' post-industrial ' world. Ernst Haas, among others, has suggested that ' culturally, the world may very well become more and more " sensate", preoccupied with empirical perception, secular, humanistic, utilitarian and hedonistic '. Thus, ' as accepted values erode we can no longer expect a consensus on such notions as the " national interest "; perhaps the post-industrial [state] will no longer be an object of value to its citizens at all '.[21]

There are already signs of such a world, at least in some industrialized countries. Those young Americans who try to escape from military service perhaps do so as much from a desire to pursue what they perceive as the ' good life ' as from

---

[20] See his *End of an Illusion: Critical Analysis of the Cold War Alliances* (London, 1969), p. 74.

[21] *Future Worlds and Present International Organizations: Some Dilemmas* (Berkeley, Inst. of Internat. Studies, 1969), pp. 6 & 8; see also Herman Kahn & Anthony Wiener, *The Year 2000* (New York, 1967).

moral scruples regarding the justness of the United States' involvement in Vietnam. Throughout the Western world generally, many of the younger generation and also some of their elders appear to find it increasingly difficult to identify themselves with the interests of their particular state. To many the state, or rather the central government, is seen as a distant bureaucratic machine unable to arouse patriotic sentiments. Would young Oxbridge, for example, now actually fight and if necessary die for ' Queen and Country ' except under severe compulsion? What will be the perception of security when these young people eventually become policy-makers? Future views of security may well differ radically from those generally held today.

It is also possible that future policy-makers may be forced to place greater emphasis on internal rather than external security. In some parts of the world internal security problems are in fact the most pressing. Some African policy-makers are fortunate in having to contend with few if any credible and immediate external threats, but they inherited fragile state structures which compel them to pay great attention to internal security. In some of the longer-established industrial-ized states, internal security is also assuming a growing importance because of the activities of protest groups able and willing to use violence in pursuing their objectives. The student riots in, say, France and Japan or the race riots in the United States could well be another sign of things to come. The industrialized states might become more unstable because of the violent methods of protest groups unable to identify themselves with the established order. Will the possible technological bureaucracy of the future, in fact, result in a reversal of Orwell's *1984*?

Finally, is there an indivisible world security, apart from the actual physical survival of the Earth itself? Almost certainly not. The agglomeration of the separate military and economic security interests of the 140 or so states is not a unity. The military security of Communist China, for example, can be regarded as militating against that of both the Soviet Union and the United States. Similarly, the economic security of Japan to some extent causes economic insecurity in Western

Europe. More significantly, perhaps, the economic interests of the poor non-white peoples are not easily identifiable with those of the rich white peoples. Nor within each of these general categories are there many identifiable common security interests in either the economic or the military sense. After all, the window on the world from Tunbridge Wells is very unlike that from Manila!

II. Models for Security by Collaboration

Despite all the qualifications which have been made, the survival of the state has been and continues to be the most important single core value perceived by statesmen and other opinion-makers. The primary safeguard of that value, moreover, is usually the possession of and if necessary the exercise of military power by a state. There are two principal strategies whereby states endeavour to preserve their security—by unilateral actions and by actions in combination with and through collaboration with other states. If either strategy were developed to its ultimate potential, the international system concerned would cease to be one composed of states.

If the first strategy were so developed, the system would be transformed into an ' empire '. If this empire were local or regional and in contact with other systems, the new political unit itself would have the choice of unilateralist or collaborative strategies for preserving external security. If the system were completely isolated or a global one, only internal security would be required. So far no state has created a world empire through world conquest, and it is inconceivable that any will do so in the foreseeable future. Even if either the Soviet Union or the United States achieved unchallengeable nuclear supremacy, in practice its security could not be absolute so long as other states remained in existence. The cost of creating a world empire by destroying or abolishing rival states would be too high, and in the unlikely event of this being achieved, the new unit itself would present unmanageable problems of government. While China and Rome conquered and transformed their international systems, their empires later collapsed through combinations of internal stresses and the pressures of other organized political units from without the system.

They did not, or rather could not, maximize their strategies of conquest to achieve the ultimate goal of a stable universal empire.

If the second strategy were maximized by the co-operative efforts of all the states within a particular international system, this new political unit would also have no external security problems unless in contact with other international systems, when it too would have a further choice of strategies. If the strategy were maximized at the global level, the result would be World Government. In theory the form of such a government could be federal, unitary, or some combination of them. The federal model would be the more practical as the unitary one would almost certainly be faced with such unmanageable administrative problems that it would collapse. All World Government models would probably require ' the establishment of an authority which takes away from [states], . . . not only the machinery of battle that can wage war, but the machinery of decision that can start a war '.[22] Such an authority is at the moment no more than an ideal dream and few if any statesmen have given it serious consideration. Only the future can tell whether such a government will be necessary for world survival. Statesmen have given considerable attention to less extreme forms of collaborative security, but before examining these it is necessary to look briefly at the unilateral efforts by states to achieve security.

Unilateralist Strategies

Unilateralism is essentially an attempt by a state to preserve security values by its own efforts alone. Success depends upon its self-sufficiency, the nature of the international system in which it exists, its geographical position *vis-à-vis* other states, and their strategies for security and relative power positions —the success of collaborative strategies also depend on similar factors. The two principal forms of the unilateralist strategy are interventionism and isolationism. Self-abnegation does not come into the unilateralist category, as the survival and other security values of any state pursuing such a strategy would be a function of the will and power of other states rather than its own efforts.

[22] See Norman Cousins, *In Place of Folly* (New York, 1961), p. 99.

The opposite of self-abnegation, the search for hegemony within an international system, represents the maximization of interventionism. Such a strategy falls short of the pursuit of ' empire ' in that other states would be permitted to remain in existence, although subordinate to the will of the dominant state in matters of high policy. Their status would be that of client or vassal states. Some of them might also be 'jackal' states—states who collaborate with the dominant state in order to pursue their independent objectives *vis-à-vis* third states under its protective cloak but still subordinate to its will. If a serious rival to the dominant state should emerge, then a balance of power would come into existence. Buffer states could also then play a part in preserving some semblance of the hegemonic system by demarcating the respective spheres of domination. The system itself, however, would cease to be hegemonic unless there were no, or at least minimal, contact between the two dominant states. In effect, unless the original system divided into two distinct international systems, a simple balance of power would come into existence.

No state has ever achieved hegemony within the global system, but many have done so within their local or regional systems. But in the case of Napoleonic France's mastery of Europe, the European system of that time was almost synonymous with the global one. However, as is almost always so with hegemonic systems, that mastery was neither absolute nor permanent. The duration of such systems has varied enormously. Nazi Germany's domination of most of Europe lasted for only a few years, but the dominant position of the United States in the Western hemisphere dates from about the end of the American Civil War in 1865, and is perhaps the most notable example in modern times of a durable and stable hegemony. Even this American hegemony has been challenged, and was a function of the hemisphere's relative geographical isolation and the self-restraint of the European powers as much as the efforts of the United States. While the system as a whole can be described as hegemonic, the parts were also characterized by collaborative security strategies on the part of the component states. The regional system itself, moreover, formed part of a larger international order based on strategies of alignment.

The contemporary technological revolution and the tremendous expenditure of resources now required to a large extent counteract efforts to achieve regional, if not local, military hegemony. Even the United States and the Soviet Union are experiencing more and more difficulty in maintaining domination of Latin America and Eastern Europe respectively. Limited interventionist strategies themselves are also both rarer and a less effective means for safeguarding security values at all levels. Some form of collaboration, explicit or implicit, with other states is unavoidable even for the superpowers, although not necessarily with each other. Indeed, almost all states are now largely dependent on other states for their military security and even more so for economic security. The Cobden thesis of world order through world trade may not be tenable, but states are much more economically interdependent than formerly. In fact, the future might well demonstrate the validity of David Mitrany's functionalist thesis of international order through economic and social co-operation by states. His thesis, essentially a more sophisticated version of Richard Cobden's one, is already valid at the Western European regional level, if not yet so at the global level he originally postulated.[23]

Isolationism, the alternative unilateralist strategy, is an even less practical means for safeguarding security values in the modern world. Like interventionism, it usually implies neither reliance on commitments by other states to assist in safeguarding security nor willingness to give such commitments to other states. But interventionism explicitly implies some degree of participation in the affairs of the local, regional, or global system, whereas isolationism keeps transactions with other states to a minimum.

In the past isolationist states have usually been self-sufficient in what they have perceived as security requirements. Geographical barriers like barren terrain, high surrounding mountains, or wide uncharted seas have been indispensable requirements for successful isolationist policies. These barriers formerly provided states such as Nepal with a natural isolation in the absence of a believed threat to military, economic, or

[23] See his *A Working Peace System* (London, 1946).

other security values. Other states such as Japan utilized natural barriers when deliberately adopting isolationist policies as a means of avoiding an actual or potential security threat. Withdrawal from one international system—global, regional, or local—does not necessarily imply withdrawal from all international systems. For example, with temporary lapses, the United States adopted a policy of abstaining from involvement in European affairs from the end of the American War of Independence until roughly the Japanese attack on Pearl Harbour in 1941, but as has already been pointed out, for much of this time she pursued an interventionist strategy in the Western hemisphere.

The contemporary revolutions in communications and technology have considerably reduced the feasibility of isolationist strategies. Not even the most powerful states can now be wholly independent of decisions made in other states. They will be affected by them to a greater or lesser extent, depending on the importance of the decision, the self-sufficiency of the state in question, and the relative power of other states. Even geographically isolated states like Tibet, who formerly had a negligible contact with all other states, have been unable to insulate themselves. Similarly, Nepalese isolation now depends more on the security values of other states than on the Himalayas. Isolation from the global system is also more difficult, as regional and local issues sometimes merge with or are intimately linked with larger issues. For example, the Yemeni civil war was of intense interest to the rival Arab groupings, whose affairs in turn were of concern to the super-powers. Nevertheless, the relationship between so-called third-world security problems and the global strategies of the super-powers is often probably not as close as some commentators maintain.

A sub-category of isolationism, neutrality, is also now not so effective a strategy for security as it previously was. In terms of international law, neutrality refers to the legal status of states who during a war play no part in the contest itself, but continue to have pacific intercourse with both sets of belligerents. The word is also widely used to describe the policy orientation of states like Sweden and Switzerland who traditionally tried to avoid involvement in the wars of other states by maintaining a strict impartiality in peacetime. Their strategies of neutrality were similar to isolationist ones in usually being passive and non-interventionist. Geographical isolation was often also important, but the preservation of their neutrality depended more on their own power and/or the self-restraint of other states. Some neutrals, like Sweden, voluntarily adopted such a strategy, others, like Austria and Laos, had it imposed on them by treaty agreements between the great powers, and some originally neutralized by treaty have voluntarily retained that status—as has Switzerland since the Congress of Vienna.

Very few of the traditional European neutrals have been able or even willing to retain that status. Switzerland, for example, although refusing to join the Western alliance system, like the European members of NATO, is dependent on the United States for much of her military security. The same is true of Eire and Sweden, who in addition now have much less passive foreign policies due to their membership of the UN. The wider perspective afforded by UN membership means that they at least have to cast votes in the General Assembly on issues not of immediate concern to them. It has also given them the opportunity to play a more active role in world affairs through participation in such activities as UN peace-keeping operations and multilateral aid programmes. Of perhaps even greater significance is the fact that all three states are integral parts of the Western economic system. Non-European neutrals like Laos have had their neutrality severely undermined or even violated by the rival ambitions of their neighbours and the great powers. Indeed, in the present era of ideological conflict and undeclared wars, the legal status of neutrality itself is much less meaningful than it was formerly. Finally, even in the past some neutral states were by no means impartial in time of war. Although officially a non-belligerent during the first two years of the Second World War, for example, the United States undertook policies heavily weighted on the side of Britain and France.

The contemporary strategies for security of states like Eire and Sweden closely resemble those of the so-called neutralist

Afro-Asian states. These states are non-aligned in that they refuse either to join the American and the Soviet cold-war alliances or to support either super-power on all diplomatic issues. They will, however, lend support to both on particular issues. Their strategy of neutralism is not isolationist, but is marked by a desire to play an active role in world affairs and the leading roles in the affairs of their own regional and local systems. Their overall strategy is best seen as one of limited intervention. Some but by no means all of them have sought to become a third force between the opposing American and Soviet cold-war camps. Their individual stands on cold-war issues have not been characterized by mutual coherence and homogeneity— they have ranged from pro-American to pro-Soviet.

As a group, their main concern has been with the evils of Western European colonialism rather than cold-war issues as such. While even the most powerful African and Asian neutralists have been unable to take much direct action themselves to hasten the decolonization process, their collective voices, and especially their combined voting strength in the General Assembly, have contributed towards undermining the ideological and practical *raison d'être* of Western European colonial rule. This role has been primarily a function of collaboration at the UN. Individually they possess little influence, but collectively they have made at least an important vocal impact at the UN. Their strategy perforce has had to be collaborative rather than unilateral. Whether or not they have had much influence on events outside the UN generally, and on the overall global balance of power in particular, is, of course, another matter.

The Africans and Asians, like the Latin Americans, now tend to concentrate more on their local and/or regional affairs than global ones as such. The death or overthrow of prominent neutralist leaders like Prime Minister Nehru and Presidents Nkrumah and Sukarno has contributed towards this relative withdrawal from global affairs. Many African and Asian leaders, however, have always preferred to concentrate on the tasks of creating modern and viable states rather than attempting to play dramatic roles in global affairs. The Afro-Asian group as a whole, moreover, is now considerably more disunited even on colonial issues than in the early 1960s. Like all unilateral strategies for security, neutralism seemingly belongs more to the past than to the future.

The Balance of Power

The balance of power has probably been the subject of more confused comment and controversy than any other concept relevant to the study of international relations. Some great philosophers of the past, like David Hume, have contributed erudite essays on the subject, and today it is of primary concern to members of the ' realist ' school of international politics, like Hans Morgenthau. Most commentators agree that the concept is associated with the emergence of the European state system, but their consensus often goes no further. Some have held it in great esteem and others have condemned it as no more than a cliché: ' a mere chimera— creation of the politician's brain—a phantasm, without definite form or tangible existence—a mere conjunction of syllables, forming words which convey sound without meaning '.[24] The disagreement stems in part from the fact that different commentators interpret and define the concept in different ways. Nearly fifty years ago, A. F. Pollard pointed out that ' the balance of power may mean almost anything; and it is used not only in different senses by different people, or in different senses by the same people at different times, but in different senses by the same person at the same time '.[25] In fact, ' the trouble with the balance of power is not that it has no meaning, but that it has too many meanings '.[26] In addition to its possible meanings and usages in the terminology of international relations, balance of power also has separate meanings and usages regarding the internal politics of states.

[24] Richard Cobden's opinion. Cited in Arnold Wolfers & Laurence Martin, eds., *The Anglo-American Tradition in Foreign Affairs* (New Haven,1956), p. 203.

[25] See A. F. Pollard, ' The Balance of Power ', *Journal of British Inst. of Internat. Affairs*, Mar. 1923, p. 58. More recently, Inis Claude and Ernst Haas, among others, have also emphasized this point. For Professor Claude's views, see *Power & Internat. Relations*, chs 2 & 3. For those of Professor Haas, see his ' The Balance of Power: Prescription, Concept, or Propaganda? ', *World Politics*, July 1953, pp. 442–77.

[26] *Power & Internat. Relations*, p. 13. Martin Wight, for example, has isolated nine distinct meanings. See his chapter ' The Balance of Power ' in Herbert Butterfield & Martin Wight, eds., *Diplomatic Investigations* (London, 1966).

The concept is also unsatisfactory as a tool for investigating collaborative strategies for security since balance-of-power models can exist alongside or be part of unilateralist and/or collective-security strategies. The models themselves can refer to simple or multiple balances between individual states or states co-operating within alliance frameworks. Some contemporary alliances are much more rigid and institutionalized than either other modern ones or those of the past. The various balance-of-power models can be operative in local, regional, and global systems; sometimes with and sometimes without links between the balances operating at the different international levels. There can also be a balance-of-power strategy at one level linked to a unilateralist or collective-security strategy at another level. Occasionally the balances within states themselves are directly related to larger international balances. The relatively static or dynamic character of particular international systems impinges on the balance-of-power processes. The systems can also change from being static to dynamic and vice versa.

The nature of the balancing process itself presents difficult problems. Is the process automatic in the sense of either mechanical or biological laws—operative without actually being willed by policy-makers? Alternatively, is it a function of the will and/or the actions of policy-makers—in other words, is it manually operated? Or is it some mixture of the automatic and the actions of policy-makers? The manually-operated view is perhaps the most tenable, although this is not to imply that policy-makers base their actions on rational calculations of what they perceive as the desirable balance. Even if they actually did this, their perceptions of that balance would almost certainly differ. The only assumption made in adopting the manually-operated view is that balancing processes depend on the disparate actions of policy-makers. The actions themselves are mostly responses to particular policy problems or combinations of them rather than to abstract calculations.

More significantly, is the actual balance-of-power process itself one of equilibrium in the sense of a roughly equal distribution of power among the states within a system? The proponents of this view base their arguments essentially on the premise that if equilibrium is disturbed at any point within the system, compensatory adjustments also occur. But was there an equal distribution of power in the first place? And are the compensatory adjustments sufficient to restore the original relative power distribution? An alternative and paradoxical view is that the process itself is one of dis-equilibrium. In other words, the relative power of the states concerned is not in actual balance. Here the basic assumption is that policy-makers usually desire a margin of power in favour of their particular state. In effect, they desire an imbalance rather than a balance. The realist school, in particular, stresses the importance of this consideration: ' the balance desired is the one which neutralizes other states, leaving the home state free to be the deciding force and the deciding voice '.[27] But is there in fact such a struggle for power either in all international systems or in the same international system all the time?

Although the modern world is characterized by great inequalities of power and an inherent dynamism, balance of power in equilibrium is the most useful means of denoting contemporary and possible future strategies for security. The process is generally in equilibrium in that the territorial integrity and physical survival of states are not usually in question. The global balance of terror between the two super-powers is also important,[28] but perhaps not as important as their involvement or interest in most conflict situations at the local and regional levels. For example, while there is by no means an equal distribution of power between the Arab states and Israel, it is highly probable that neither the Soviet Union nor the United States would permit either side to obtain, still less to retain, an absolute power margin in its favour. This is not to imply that the super-powers, individually or collectively, are able and willing to *manage* the situation. The argument is merely that they act as guarantors of the dis-putant's actual physical survival as sovereign states. But

[27] See Nicholas Spykman, *America's Strategy in World Politics* (1942), cited in Sprout, *Foundations of Internat. Politics*, p. 117.

[28] The implications of the balance of terror are discussed on pp. 28–30.

American and Soviet guarantees are essentially a function both of their perception of the degree to which their own interests are involved and their actual ability to intervene successfully. Neither attempted to oppose Communist China's annexation of Tibet, and it is improbable that they would guarantee the survival of white South Africa in the unlikely event of the Black African states achieving and utilizing an absolute military superiority.

Ideological disequilibrium can occur. In some areas the nature of the governmental processes and the ideological orientation of states have fluctuated, sometimes drastically. The point is well demonstrated by the position in Iraq since the overthrow of General Nuri al-Said and the Hashimite dynasty in 1958 and in Cuba after the ousting of the Batista regime. The fluctuations result as much from internal factors as from external pressures, and the super-powers rarely take a direct or open part in them. Within the cores of the American and Russian spheres of influence, ideological orientations are much more stable. Czechoslovakia, not Cuba, remains the norm.

The simple balance-of-power model in equilibrium primarily refers to a stable bipolar situation in which either two states, two groups of states, or one state and a group of states confront each other. In theory the strategies for security of all single states involved in this model are essentially unilateralist as security values are safeguarded primarily by their own efforts alone. It is unusual, however, for only two groups to be involved at either the local, regional, or global levels. Even if the balance is primarily the concern of two groups only, third parties will usually have an interest, direct or indirect, in that balance. For example, the confrontation between Israel and the Arab states is of acute interest to the two super-powers whose supply of arms directly affects the power distribution in the region. Other international actors, like France and the UN, have also played important roles in the balancing process.

Hugh Seton-Watson among others has argued that after the Second World War there emerged a bipolar balance at the global level between the Soviet Union and the United States. He admitted that 'the old Great Powers of Western Europe are still factors to be reckoned with' and that China and India ' are capable of reaching giant power status within a few decades ', but maintained that ' the two giants of today overshadow the world in a manner that is new in human history '.[29] Was there, in fact, really a simple global balance even during the height of the cold war? The United States was neither able nor desirous of having the same tight control over NATO as the Soviet Union had over the Warsaw Pact. In the 1960s the Americans became increasingly frustrated by French inflexibility and found little support from their European allies regarding such non-European issues as the Vietnam conflict. Even the Soviet Union's mastery of Eastern Europe was less than absolute. While managing to retain overall control, she was unable to prevent Yugoslavia from breaking away or Rumania from acquiring at least a partial freedom of manoeuvre. There was only a simple balance to the extent that the military superiority of the two super-powers was the most important factor in ensuring overall European stability.

While there might have been a comparatively simple European equilibrium between the two super-powers at the height of the cold war, this was not the case globally. During the 1950s especially, the United States was the only super-power to adopt even a partial overall global strategy for security. The Soviet Union was much more limited in her horizons. Russian policy-makers mostly confined their efforts to stabilizing control over Eastern Europe and to extending Soviet influence in areas adjacent to the Communist world. The widening of the Soviet Union's global horizons has not resulted in an overall simple equilibrium. The influence of the Soviet Union and the United States has fluctuated in such disputed peripheral areas as the Middle East, neither has shown much concern in obtaining preponderant influence in Africa south of the Sahara nor made significant inroads into the other's regional heartlands. Russian influence in Cuba has itself not seriously undermined American hegemony in the Western hemisphere—the advent and survival of the Castro regime owes more to the limitations and self-restraint of American power than to Russian support.

[29] See Hugh Seton-Watson, *Neither War nor Peace* (London, 1960), p. 9.

The emergence of Communist China as a potential super-power has been an important factor undermining a bipolar world. China is still essentially an Asian regional power rather than a global one, but the Soviet Union and the United States have to take into consideration her increased influence in such states as Syria and Tanzania. In much of South-east Asia Chinese influence is as great if not greater than theirs. American policy-makers now regard China rather than the Soviet Union as the principal adversary of the United States in the region. In particular, they perceive the major threat to American interests as not so much Soviet assistance to Hanoi as possibly unlimited Chinese intervention if the conflict in Indo-China should escalate still further.[30] For their part, the Russians have been unable either to control China or to prevent the initiative, if not the mastery of international Communism, shifting from Moscow to Peking. But China's role even in Asia should not be unduly emphasized. Her overt influence is limited in such countries as Japan, Malaysia, and Indonesia under the Suharto regime, and, of course, Japan is the dominant power in economic terms.

The global balance has in fact been largely multiple rather than simple, especially in so far as it is an amalgam of various local and regional power configurations. The interests of the traditional Western European colonial powers in their former empires and spheres of influence have not always been identical with those of the United States—witness the sharp American reaction to the Anglo-French Suez adventure of 1956. The French arms deal with Libya announced in January 1970 undermined American efforts at least partially to stabilize the Arab-Israeli conflict by reducing the supply of arms. Britain and France themselves have been rivals in the Middle East and other areas of the third world, their rivalry often being independent of super-power conflicts of interest. The super-powers have also had to contend with a general desire by the African and Asian peoples themselves to have the ultimate say in their own local and regional affairs. Globally,

---

[30] Eventual unlimited Chinese intervention cannot be wholly discounted, but both the Americans and the Chinese have so far been much more circumspect than was the case during the Korean War.

throughout most of the 1950s and the 1960s, some Afro-Asian states, with differing degrees of emphasis, tried to act as a ' third force ' between the super-powers. On the whole their efforts, like the various British attempts at bridge-building, met with only limited success. They made some contribution towards creating a favourable climate for East-West negotiation and *détente*, but on major questions like non-proliferation and the Strategic Arms Limitation Talks (SALT), the super-powers preferred to deal directly with each other, without interference from possibly meddlesome outsiders.

In one respect only is the overall contemporary global system really characterized by a simple equilibrium balance. The Soviet Union and the United States possess an overwhelming superiority in terms of weapons of mass destruction. Their balance of terror makes for equilibrium in that neither can be completely certain of physically surviving a full-scale nuclear conflict. Their mutual destructive capacity is such that quantitative advantages do not really result in qualitative ones. If in the foreseeable future one obtained a marked advantage through developments in weapons of mass destruction and/or more effective anti-ballistic missile systems, these are unlikely to alter the existing balance unduly. There might well be very unsettling effects, but there is likely to be restraint in that the one with the advantage could not be wholly confident of its impregnability generally or of its ability to knock out the other's nuclear capacity on a first strike. If only a few missiles survived, they would probably be sufficient to inflict an unacceptable level of destruction. The advent of Polaris-type submarines and solid-fuel missiles with multiple warheads further reduces vulnerability to first strikes.

Even so, such commentators as Herman Kahn and Henry Kissinger developed theoretical strategies for controlling nuclear conflict and went so far as to moot the possibility of city swapping.[31]   Such blueprints and conjectures are perhaps of little more than academic interest, although their inherent inhumanity

[31] See Herman Kahn, *Thinking About the Unthinkable* (New York, 1962), and Henry Kissinger, *Nuclear Weapons and Foreign Policy* (New York, 1957).   Dr Kissinger, of course, is currently a leading adviser of the Nixon Administration and his earlier views have become modified with time and greater practical responsibility.

is horrifying.   The contingency of nuclear war by accident or miscalculation is hopefully considered improbable and is at least publicly discounted by the Soviet Union and the United States. This in itself is not wholly reassuring, but both appear to be anxious to maintain the most stringent safeguards, and their mutual hot line suggests a desire to reduce the likelihood of a pre-emptive strike.   While their nuclear stalemate has not eliminated the tension between them or significantly reduced the pace of their nuclear arms race, the SALT discussions indicate a concern to diminish arms expenditure, or at least to try to avoid the big increase entailed in constructing effective anti-ballistic missile systems.

The balance of terror has so far been a factor in restraining the Soviet Union and the United States from settling their disputes by force of arms in what are perceived as vital areas like Central Europe, or from directly confronting each other in more peripheral ones. The degree of security which this balance has given to the Western European states has not been openly recognized, nor is it acceptable to all of them.[32] In particular, Gaullist France was psychologically unable to accept the second-class power status coincidental with military security afforded by the United States' nuclear deterrent or to entrust her security wholly to that deterrent.[33] But France's endeavours to become another third force independent of both super-powers has not really undermined the existing balance of terror. The first and even second strike viabilities of both the French *force de frappe* and the British so-called independent nuclear deterrent, alone or collectively, remain doubtful. Gaullist initiative was essentially by courtesy of the American nuclear umbrella.

China's accession to the nuclear club has not so far seriously altered the balance of terror. She has put her first satellite into orbit, but Chinese nuclear weapons will probably remain

[32] Paradoxically, the security afforded to the European states by the American and Soviet nuclear balance is not wholly dissimilar from the security afforded to small states like Belgium by the simple and multiple equilibrium balances among the European great powers during the nineteenth century.

[33] The decision to create *la force de frappe* was, of course taken under the Fourth, not the Fifth, French Republic. For de Gaulle's views, see Forum, *Pour ou contre la Force de frappe* (Paris, 1963).

very vulnerable to a first strike attack for a few years at least —though her delivery systems are probably or soon will be sophisticated enough seriously to threaten the Soviet Union and the west coast of the United States. Within China's immediate geographical proximity, especially in South-east Asia, however, Chinese nuclear weapons will probably be very important in the near future. The global balance if and when China obtains a viable nuclear weapons system can only be a matter of conjecture, although some theoretical assumptions may be made by drawing on evidence provided by historical precedents and recent Chinese external policies. While there has been a good deal of Russian and Western disquiet regarding Chinese ambitions, she has so far been restrained in practice, if not in her public policy declarations. In fact a misleading picture of an aggressive China has probably been painted, largely thanks to a combination of American and Russian propaganda, the recent activities of the Red Guards, and China's failure to observe accepted diplomatic courtesies. She annexed Tibet, over which there was a long-established Chinese claim to suzerainty, but apparently had only limited objectives in the Sino-Indian war of 1962, and has so far shown great forbearance regarding American activities in Indo-China. Consequently it is by no means certain that the balance of terror would become one of dis-equilibrium due to her aggressive ambitions if China joined the super-power nuclear club.

In that event the balance would almost certainly become a multiple one. This would be the case even if either China, or the Soviet Union, or the United States attempted to act as the nuclear balancer between the other two. When, in the nineteenth-century European system, Britain attempted to remain aloof from Continental entanglements and to act as a balancer, placing her weight on the side of what appeared to be the weakest grouping, she was in fact assuming an active role in the balancing process. The balance model itself was thereby transformed from a simple to a multiple one. The British reluctance to become committed to any European group would almost certainly be repeated, *mutatis mutandis*, by the nuclear giants of the future. And in the future it is not impossible that there might be an effective Western European nuclear capacity, to complicate matters still further. In discussing the implications of British membership of the European Communities, the Conservative Party's Bow Group among others has outlined the prospects for a viable Western European nuclear deterrent.[34] Only time can tell whether it could or would be independent of the American nuclear arsenal.

Finally, traditional perceptions of the balance-of-power concept themselves are of relatively limited use for understanding some contemporary strategies for security. In North America and Western Europe especially, balance of power conceived in military terms is not very helpful in the context of American-Canadian relations or those of the member states of the EEC. In these cases it is economic, not military, balances which are crucial. Indeed, within the Europe of the Six, erstwhile enemies have adopted a collaborative strategy, not so much to seek an internal balance as to integrate their national economies and pursue common policies. While this is by no means the case globally, economic rather than military and political balances are becoming more and more important. Balances of aid and trade are now sometimes more relevant than military balances of power.

Collective Security

To a large extent the intellectual and emotional appeal which collective security has for many in the modern world dates from the horrors of the First World War. The latter was widely believed to have conclusively demonstrated the ineffectiveness of European balance-of-power systems for providing security. This belief was coincidental with the growth of nationalist thought emphasizing mankind's essential unity and the view that war was too crude and, indeed, too stupid a method for settling disputes between states. Collective security's intellectual origins primarily derive from European thought and experience—from the schemes for perpetual peace of such thinkers as Pierre Dubois, the Abbé St Pierre,

[34] See *Our Future in Europe* (London, Feb. 1970), pp. 9–16.

the Duc de Sully, and Immanuel Kant, while the nineteenth-century Concert of Europe afforded a more practical model.[35]

Unlike the balance of power, collective security is comparatively easy to define. Inis Claude aptly states that it

involves the creation of an international system in which the danger of aggressive warfare by any states is to be met by the avowed determination of virtually all other states to exert pressure of every necessary variety—moral, diplomatic, economic, and military—to frustrate attack upon any state.

The strategy is collective in the fullest sense as ' it purports to provide security for *all* states, *by* the action of all states, *against* all states which might challenge the existing order by the arbitrary unleashing of their power '.[36]

This three musketeers' strategy of ' one for all and all for one ' has certain striking similarities with the balance of power. Both are based on deterrence and inherently assume rational behaviour by policy-makers acting to safeguard the interests of their states through the preservation of the international system as a whole. Both also involve the paradox of war for peace—peace being achieved through the collective capacity and will to resist. Coincidental with this fundamental preoccupation with military power, there is a mistrust of any state with an undue preponderance, though collective security focuses on aggressive *policy*, whereas balance of power is more concerned with aggressive *capacity*.

The divergences between the two strategies are even more striking. Collective security denotes a general alliance eliminating ' the pattern of competitive alignments ' characteristic of the balance system. It calls for an alliance uniting states ' in defence of the order of the community, instead of one which divides them into antagonistic groups, jockeying for position against each other '. It is *inward looking*, whereas balance of power involves ' essentially *externally oriented* groupings '. In fact, whereas the latter ' postulates two or more worlds in jealous confrontation . . . collective security postulates

---

[35] For a fuller exposition of the European ancestry of collective security, see F. H. Hinsley, *Power and the Pursuit of Peace* (London, 1963).

[36] *Power & Internat. Relations*, p. 110. The examination of collective security in this section is largely based on the author's understanding of Professor Claude's work on the subject.

one world, organized for the cooperative maintenance of order within its bounds'. One promotes 'order through the arrangement of appropriate patterns of conflictual relations', the other requires 'a structure of general cooperation to hold conflict in check'. Balance of power 'emphasizes the manipulation of rivalry' with 'competitive struggle' being 'dealt with by the realization of cooperative arrangements within limited groupings'. Collective security, however, stresses 'the exploitation of cooperative potential' in a system where 'outbreaks of sharp conflict . . . are ranked as occasional phenomena' rather than the standard norm. 'The former promises competitive security while the latter promises cooperative security'. One leaves latitude for '*ad hoc* calculation' of what is required whereas the other assumes the indivisibility of peace. In other words, 'collective security decrees a set response in support of any victim of aggression; balance of power confirms the freedom of the state to pick and choose'.[37]

The subjective and objective requirements of collective security are such that it has not so far been institutionalized at the global level and is unlikely to be so in the foreseeable future.[38] Certainly, the practice of neither the League of Nations nor of the UN conforms to the collective-security ideal. This postulate is, of course, contrary to the view of some of their respective founding fathers and many commentators of the time. Indeed, to many, the League's collective-security provisions—Articles x–xvi—were the heart of the Covenant. Article x, in fact, was central to the whole ethos of the League as an instrument for safeguarding international security. It laid down that all

Members of the League undertake to respect and preserve as against external aggression the territorial integrity and existing political independence of all Members of the League. In case of any such aggression or in case of any threat of danger of such aggression, the Council shall advise upon the means by which this obligation shall be fulfilled.

Unfortunately, however, the League Council was hamstrung

[37] Claude, *Power & Internat. Relations*, pp. 144–6.

[38] For a full and cogent examination of these subjective and objective requirements, see Claude's *Swords into Plowshares* (New York, 1964), ch. 12.

34 INTERNATIONAL SECURITY

by the unanimity rule, and the requisite machinery for collective action was either non-existent or, when it existed, ineffectual. Moreover, as Charles Manning and others have pointed out, the League failed as a security club because its leading members, Britain and France, did not possess the will or the ability to resist German, Italian, and Japanese aggression during the 1930s.[39] The anti-*status-quo* ambitions of the Axis states were contrary to the implicit collective-security assumption of an essentially *status-quo* international system. While there was some attempt to fulfil another of its requirements, disarmament or at least a measure of arms control, this was also ineffectual—many of the more important negotiations in fact were conducted outside the League's auspices. Perhaps most significant of all, many of the great powers were not League members for all or even part of the time. In particular, although the League's very existence had owed so much to President Woodrow Wilson, the fact that the United States never joined was probably crucial. The United States' failure to identify herself with the League undermined the one notable League attempt at collective action—the feeble endeavour to restrain Italy's attack on Ethiopia through collective sanctions was meaningless without American consent to curtail oil supplies. In fact, the half-hearted and indecisive League effort itself can be traced ' to the facts that the League was, in an important sense, a European regional organization, and that its leading European members were more strongly motivated by considerations related to the pattern of political combinations in Europe than by commitment to the general principle of collective security '.[40]

The UN was designed to be a more effective instrument of international security than the League. Whereas the Covenant ruled against *illegal* war only, the Charter was intended to prohibit all aggressive acts by states. The Organization's security ideal was set out in Article 2 (4) of the Charter: ' All members shall refrain in their international relations from the threat of force or use of force against the territorial

[39] See C. A. W. Manning, ' The " Failure " of the League of Nations ', *Agenda*, i/1 (1942), reproduced in Cosgrove & Twitchett, *New Internat. Actors*, pp. 105–23.
[40] See Claude, *European Organisation in the Global Context* (Brussels, 1965), p. 8.

integrity or political independence of any state, or in any other manner inconsistent with the Purposes of the United Nations'. Article 2 (3) emphasized that members should settle their disputes by peaceful means, and Chapter VI of the Charter defined the Organization's role in this process.[41] Under Chapter VII the Security Council was vested with the authority to order, nor merely to recommend, collective mandatory sanctions against actual or potential aggressors.[42] its role in these processes was underlined by combining the words 'security' and 'council' in its title. Article 47 made provision for a Military Staff Committee to assist and advise the Council on the measures to be taken. In addition to its institutional advantages over the League, in some respects at least the UN has operated in an international atmosphere more favourable to the collective-security ideal. The large states are now not so prone to undertake direct aggressive war for territorial gains as were the Axis states during the 1930s.[43]

The overall international climate and division of power, however, militate against the practice of the collective-security ideal. The ideological nature of many contemporary international disputes, whether in the form of so-called Communist versus capitalist or colonialist versus anti-colonialist, usually results in states adopting rigid postures alien to collective-security requirements. The nature and scope of much modern conflict is another unfavourable development. Subversion and guerrilla-type warfare are not as susceptible as formally declared or rather traditional-type wars to collective action. When the latter occur, moreover, it is often difficult if not impossible to discern the actual aggressors. Who, for example, was responsible for the Six-Day War of July 1967, Egypt or Israel? The most important contemporary international development militating against collective-security requirements is the tremendous military power possessed by the two super-powers and China. No state or combination of states can

[41] Arts 33-8.
[42] Arts 39-51.
[43] Alan James elucidates the contemporary anti-annexationist ethos in ch. 3 below. The international security functions of the UN are so ably and comprehensively examined by him that my investigation is relatively cursory.

seriously contemplate unlimited punitive measures against these three giants—the cost to themselves would be too great. After all, it took five to six years of major war to bring Germany and Japan to their knees. The military capabilities of the big three also provide a protective cloak for their respective client states.

The UN itself was not primarily designed as a collective-security instrument. The veto rights given to the five permanent members of the Security Council indicate that the Organization was intended to institutionalize the Allied wartime coalition in the postwar era. While this may have been realistic, it was not in accordance with the collective-security ideal. The emergence of the cold war and the consequent absence of great-power unanimity prevented significant utilization of the Security Council's actual authority regarding threats to or breaches of the peace. The Military Staff Committee never became a viable body and the General Assembly has been unable to assume the Council's intended role; either consti-tutionally under the Uniting For Peace Resolution of 1950 or in practice when the Soviet Union and the United States believed they had a vital interest in UN non-involvement. Taiwan not Peking, moreover, occupies the Chinese seat on the Security Council. The UN, of course, has performed some marginal but important international security functions, especially through its peace-keeping forces.[44] Unfortunately there is not the requisite international consensus and will for the Organization to become *the* collective-security instrument. This position is unlikely to change significantly in the fore-seeable future.[45]

In the longer term, the East–West ideological and power confrontation might not be so important a threat to interna-tional security as a possible North–South one between the rich, white peoples and the poor, non-white ones. In fact, the operations of the UN and its various specialized agencies in economic, social, and functional fields generally, possibly

[44] For an authoritative and comprehensive treatment of UN peace-keeping activities, see Alan James, *The Politics of Peace-Keeping* (London, 1969).

[45] Rhodesia's success so far in defying UN economic sanctions provides some indication of the ability of even small states to ignore UN edicts. But the Rhodesian case is perhaps a very special one.

already have more relevance to international security than their purely political and military ones. Functional-type activities were partly foreshadowed in the Covenant and gained increasing importance during the League's history, but it was only with the creation of the UN that they were recognized as of central concern. Franklin Roosevelt's various statements on basic freedoms and Cordell Hull's belief in the absolute necessity for international economic co-operation were reflected in the Charter's reference to them as among the Organization's major principles and purposes in Article I (3).[46]

Indeed, the UN's general developing role in the functional field is often regarded as its most important one and the chief hope for the future. Many African and Asian leaders often publicly state that collective global approaches represent the most desirable means for tackling endemic economic and social underdevelopment. UNCTAD and universal approaches, however, sometimes tend to overlook the problems of particular regions and the *unique* ones of individual states. In fact, some regional bodies not directly if at all within the UN's institutional orbit, have assumed, if not usurped, some of the Organization's functions.[47] The UN itself has adopted a regionally-administered approach in its Economic Commissions for Africa, Latin America, etc.

The UN's institutional nexus was designed to promote limited functional co-operation, especially economic co-operation, between developed states rather than solving the third world's problems of poverty, still less the conservation of mankind's ecological environment. Nevertheless, global co-operation is probably essential for tackling problems of air and ocean pollution. In the long term such action will probably be crucial for mankind's survival. Unfortunately, it may well be too late by the time individual states fully

[46] Art. 1 (3) states that a central objective is ' To achieve international cooperation in solving international problems of an economic, social, cultural, or humanitarian character, and in promoting and encouraging respect for human rights and for fundamental freedoms for all without distinction as to race, language, or religion '. The Economic and Social Council is, of course, listed as a principal organ of the UN—in theory it possesses institutional parity with the Security Council and the General Assembly.

[47] In particular, the EEC's various association arrangements with independent African states.

accept this and take effective collective action. The UN might well provide a useful central forum if ever such action is taken.[48]

Collective-Defence and Regional Arrangements

Many Western commentators and statesmen are apt to refer to CENTO, NATO, and SEATO as collective-security arrangements, despite the fact that they were established with specific potential enemies in view. Lester Pearson, for example, was prone to this confusion when giving the 1968 Reith Lectures.[49] In part the confusion can be regarded as an attempt, conscious or unconscious, to cloak these cold-war alliances with the idealism often associated with collective security. These defence arrangements, together with the Warsaw Pact, are primarily examples of collective defence, which itself may be defined as a specific pledge by a group of states that they will be prepared and willing to co-ordinate their actions in face of a threat to any one of them by an implicitly or explicitly determined potential aggressor or aggressors. Within such security mechanisms there is usually an attempt to define precisely both the commitments and the assistance to be expected.

Collective-defence arrangements are in essence an amalgam of collective-security and the balance-of-power ideals, with the latter predominating. The aggressor is outside rather than inside the group. There is, however, a fundamental distinction between these two types of collaborative security: former balance-of-power arrangements were usually flexible, whereas contemporary collective-defence alliances tend to be rigid and institutionalized. The difference is primarily due to a change in the nature of war. Compared with earlier times, nowadays there is a much greater ' possibility of decisive operations at the very outset of war, or even before declaration of it '. Consequently, ' plans and preparations made before the outbreak have come to be ever more important as compared with measures taken when the war is already in progress '.

[48] The UN has already begun to organize various conferences and studies on pollution and conservation problems. For a useful exposition of the problem of oceanic pollution see Mary M. Sibthorp, *Oceanic Pollution: a Survey and Some Suggestions for Control* (London, David Davies Memorial Inst., June 1969).

[49] *Peace in the Family of Man* (London, 1969), pp. 16–17.

Contingency planning is more vital in alliances if the partici-
pating states are to be able and ready to meet the initial
enemy attack with effective co-ordinated responses. Without
such preparation, the alliance could well be of only limited
value even though the commitments may be acknowledged
without delay.[50]

It is sometimes argued that collective-defence arrangements
like NATO and the Warsaw Pact are in accordance with the
provisions of the UN Charter. They are probably in line with
the legal requirements of the Charter: both Article 5 of the
North Atlantic Treaty and Article 4 of the Warsaw Pact
explicitly refer to the ' right of individual or collective self-
defence ' recognized by Article 51 of the UN Charter. It is,
however, much more debatable whether they accord with
the spirit of the Charter or are the type of regional arrangement
envisaged in 1945. In some respects they represent an attempt
to restrain a potentially resurgent Germany, but NATO and
the Warsaw Pact are essentially contrivances designed to
check possible aggression by the Soviet Union or the United
States respectively.[51] The member states of both declare that
the measures taken by them in the event of armed attack
would be reported to the Security Council and would be
terminated when the Council had taken the necessary steps
to restore and maintain international peace and security.
But the Council's role in any *hot* European conflict involving
the two super-powers would almost certainly be minimal.

While the ethos of both NATO and the Warsaw Pact contra-
dict the spirit of the UN security system and the very essence of
global collective security, they do institutionalize a desire for
collective resistance to aggression. Collective-defence organizations can also take on an internal collective-security guise.
For example, the so-called Brezhnev doctrine of limited
sovereignty for ' socialist ' states, by which the Soviet Union
justified the August 1968 invasion of Czechoslovakia, was
based on the premise that the Warsaw Pact members in

[50] See Butterfield & Wight, *Diplomatic Investigations*, ch. 8: ' Collective Security
and Military Alliances ', by G. A. Hudson, p. 176.

[51] The various ramifications of European security problems are more fully
examined by Peter Nailor in ch. 4 below.

particular, and Communist states generally, did not have the right to undertake actions which jeopardized the interests of other states of ' the socialist commonwealth '. The Brezhnev doctrine and the Warsaw Pact, however, are essentially corruptions of the collective-security and the collective-defence ideals. They merely institutionalize, if not legitimize, Russian hegemony over Eastern Europe. Procedures for consultation are at the most nominal regarding issues imping-ing on what the Soviet Union herself defines as affecting her security.[52]

In theory the inter-American system is much closer to the collective-security ideal than the Communist system in Eastern Europe. The Act of Chapultepec of 1945, the basis of the postwar inter-American system, possessed both collective-security and collective-defence characteristics. Article 3 of this declaration, on ' reciprocal assistance and American solidarity ', condemned aggression from within and from without the inter-American system. The Inter-American Treaty of Reciprocal Assistance signed at Rio in 1947 and Chapter 5 of the Charter of the Organization of American States, drawn up at Bogotá in April 1948, explicitly mentioned inter-American co-operation regarding such aggression and established institutional machinery for joint consultation. But the collective-security element was diluted if not eradicated by the 1948 Bogotá declarations condemning Communism and the existence of European colonies in the Western hemis-phere as ' irreconcilable with the traditions of the New World '. It was further diminished at the Caracas meeting of the OAS in March 1954. The ' Declaration of Solidarity for Preserva-tion of the Political Integrity of the American States against International Communist Intervention ' condemned ' the activities of international Communism as constituting inter-vention in American affairs ' and provided for collaboration by the American states ' for the purpose of counteracting the subversive activities of the international Communist movement within their respective jurisdictions '.

The collective-defence attributes of the inter-American

---

[52] For a brief but cogent examination of the Warsaw Pact, see Malcolm Mackintosh, *The Evolution of the Warsaw Pact* (London, ISS, June 1969).

system too are somewhat diluted. The economic and military preponderance of the United States is such that OAS consultative processes and inter-American co-operation usually serve only to endorse her own policy objectives. The ideological heritage of the Monroe Doctrine reinforces a preference for unilateral action regarding perceived encroachments on American hemispherical security. The United States herself defined and acted to suppress the believed Communist threats posed by the appropriation in 1954 by the Arbenz regime of the Guatemalan profits of the United Fruit Company, by the advent of the Castro regime in Cuba, and by Colonel Caamano's revolt of May 1965 in the Dominican Republic. An inter-American ' police force ' was dispatched to Santo Domingo, but only after the United States marines had achieved their primary objectives. Nevertheless, in marked contrast to the manner in which the Soviet Union exercises control over Eastern Europe, the United States at least pays considerable lip-service to inter-American consultation even on vital security issues. This is perhaps the most that can be hoped for at the present time![53]

Neither super-power has obtained unqualified alliance support for all its externally or internally oriented alliance policies. Rumania provides a classic example in refusing to take sides in the Sino-Soviet dispute and, more significantly, to acknowledge the validity of the Brezhnev doctrine. Despite vulnerability to Soviet pressure, she continues to maintain that the Warsaw Pact serves only to safeguard the external defence of its members, not to justify interference in their internal affairs.[54] The United States has experienced even more difficulty in obtaining alliance backing. In the OAS the Latin American Republics have neither consistently nor whole-heartedly endorsed her inter-American or global policies. The members of her principal cold-war alliances, CENTO, NATO, and SEATO, have been even more reluctant to

[53] For a good account of the inter-American system, see Gordon Connell-Smith, *The Inter-American System* (London, 1966).

[54] For a fuller summary of the Rumanian attitude, see *The Times*, 23 Aug. 1968. On the Soviet-Rumanian Treaty of 7 July 1970, which omits any reference to the ' protection of socialism ' (unlike the Soviet-Czechoslovak Treaty), see ibid., 9 July 1970.

give similar endorsements. This is particularly true of the responses of the members of one alliance to American policies in another alliance. The role which geographical distance can play in this failure of identification has been superbly demonstrated by Arnold Wolfers. He visualized the American alliance system as a wheel with the United States at the hub and her allies 'spread out along its rim, each occupying the end of a spoke':

Danger to any allied country—to the end of a spoke . . . is communicated to the United States at the hub as a threat to the entire wheel and it therefore elicits a correspondingly strong defensive reaction. No similar reaction can be expected, however, from countries located on the opposite spokes or on remote sections of the rim. Instead, any American military action or exercise of 'brinkmanship' on behalf of an ally in immediate danger tends to strike other more remote allies not only as a diversion of American attention and strength to tasks of minor importance, but as a risky manoeuver that may involve them all in conflicts incapable of being localized.[55]

The emergence of sophisticated mechanisms for the peaceful settlement of disputes within particular regional areas in some ways can be regarded as growing out of a fusion of the collective-security and the collective-defence ideals. Such mechanisms exist in Western Europe, the North Atlantic area generally, Latin America, the Arab world, and Black Africa.[56] In years to come, they may well evolve and even assume significant regional peace-keeping functions. In fact, there could be an argument for a resurrection and adaptation of Winston Churchill's wartime suggestion of a two-tier UN—a central Council at the global level underpinned by regional assemblies. Lester Pearson among others has recently made suggestions on these lines. In making them he pointed out that 'in the economic and social field, the practice has been growing of delegating responsibility and authority to United Nations regional commissions', but any action on these lines 'would require an amendment to the

---

[55] *Discord & Collaboration*, pp. 210–11.

[56] For a useful examination of regional mechanisms for the peaceful settlement of disputes, see David Davies Memorial Inst., *Report of a Study Group on the Peaceful Settlement of International Disputes* (London, 1966).

Charter', and ' the veto operates in respect of amendments'.[57]

Another objection to such proposals is that while they are at least theoretically realizable for Western Europe, possibly Latin America, and even Black Africa, for a long time to come they will probably be unrealizable for the Middle East and South-east Asia. In these two areas particularly, there is minimal consensus among the leading states, and the major threats to security come from within the respective regional systems themselves. In fact, neither the Arab world, still less the Middle East or South-east Asia can properly be regarded as regional systems except in a very simplified geographical sense. The widely differing historical, cultural, economic, and political norms found within them make unrealistic attempts to view either as a distinct regional system in its own right. For example, although it has performed some useful functions in furthering co-operation among the Arab states, the existence of Israel rather than inter-Arab compatibility provides the driving force holding the Arab League together. Other regions such as Western Europe may be amorphous in absolute terms, but they represent relatively much more coherent communities of interest.[58]

In fact, few contemporary regional arrangements possess ' security-community ' characteristics in the sense discerned by Karl Deutsch and his associates. They define a security community as existing when states attain a ' sense of community ' and develop ' institutions and practices strong enough to assure, for a " long " time, dependable expectations of " peaceful change " ' among them. The absence of violence is an overall priority, conflicts being resolved by conciliation and compromise rather than by force.[59] In the last few years

[57] *Peace in the Family of Man*, pp. 85–6.

[58] See further Bruce M. Russett, *International Regions and the International System* (Chicago, 1967); Peter Lyon, *War and Peace in South-East Asia* (London, 1969); Robert W. Macdonald, *The League of Arab States* (Princeton, 1965).

[59] See Karl Deutsch & others, *Political Community and the North Atlantic Area* (Princeton, 1957), p. 5. The present writer has adapted Professor Deutsch's original definition. In particular, ' states ' has been used instead of ' group of people ', and the term ' integration ' avoided altogether because of the more precise meanings given to it by other commentators. Professor Deutsch argued that security communities fall into two main categories: (1) ' pluralistic ' if no common governmental institutions have been created, and (2) 'amalgamated' if

among the member states of the Arab League, the OAS, and the Organization of African Unity, there has been open conflict and/or subversion between some of them which could easily recur in the immediate future. Neither CENTO nor SEATO can be regarded as a security community. Among the member states of both alliances there is not the required mutual compatibility of economic, political, and social values or the responsive ' sympathy-feeling ' between their respective élite groups necessary for security communities to develop. The Warsaw Pact comes nearer to fulfilling the requirements of a security community. Nevertheless, while there may be a mutual sympathy among the ruling Communist élites of its member states (itself a dubious proposition), there is probably no such perception among their peoples. Nor can the Warsaw Pact really be viewed as a community when its very existence is primarily a function of the military power and unilateral will of the Soviet Union.

NATO on the whole, however, does fulfil the tests Professor Deutsch believed necessary for a security community to develop. Compared with other organized groups of states, there is a mutual compatibility of major values between its members. Although there are some very notable exceptions, the majority of them are industrialized, liberal democracies, with a common cultural heritage derived from Greece, Rome, and Christianity. Certainly, and in marked contrast to the position a few decades ago, its members apparently do not contemplate fighting each other in the immediate future, that is with the possible exceptions of Greece and Turkey. But, as Stanley Hoffmann among others has pointed out, much more than the mere absence of violence between groups is required for the existence of a true community.[60]

Overall, NATO cannot be regarded as a true community for

a common central decision-making body of whatever type has been established. He believed that there are three ' background conditions ' necessary for a plural- istic security community to develop and ten for an amalgamated security com- munity to do so. The absence of violence is an essential prerequisite. See Deutsch, pp. 31–3, 46–58, 65–70, & 115–6.

[60] See Stanley Hoffmann, ' Discord in Community: the North Atlantic Area as a Partial International System ', in Francis O. Wilcox & H. Field Haviland, eds., *The Atlantic Community: Progress and Prospects* (New York, 1963).

three main, interrelated reasons. Amitai Etzioni has com-
mented on the tendency for military co-operation not automatically to 'spill over' into the political and economic
fields.[61] This spill-over has not really taken place within
NATO, although there has existed a highly sophisticated
degree of military co-operation and co-ordination, especially
compared with contemporary and past military alliances.
Article 2 of the North Atlantic Treaty provides for extra-
military co-operation, a significant amount of which has
occurred. But simultaneously there has been more such
co-operation between some of its member states outside the
NATO framework, particularly among the six members of the
EEC. This leads on to the second reason. There is a much
more developed and significant 'core area' among the Six
which has underlaid their progress towards actual 'supranational' integration.[62] As a group they believe—as do
NATO members like Britain who wish to join them—that their
future lies with the EEC, not with NATO or the so-called North
Atlantic area. NATO is increasingly viewed by many as an
anachronism of the cold-war era. A Soviet attack on Western
Europe is widely seen as improbable and NATO primarily
fulfils a military need only. Even the West Germans do not
believe that it can assist in furthering German reunification:
witness Chancellor Brandt's *Ostpolitik*. Indeed, although causing
disharmony in both, President de Gaulle was far more circumspect in the realm of EEC affairs than in NATO ones.

The third reason is that the members of NATO frequently
have important divergences in their military or economic
interests. American involvement in South-east Asia is not
supported by the majority of the NATO members with more
than lip-service, if that. American policies in the Middle
East, Latin America, and even Western Europe are also by
no means identical to those of the other NATO members. For
her part, the United States has been extremely suspicious of

---

[61] Amitai Etzioni has ably probed the importance of the 'spill-over' effect.
See in particular his 'The Dialectics of Supranational Unification', *American
Political Science Review*, lvi (1962).
[62] The importance and significance of the 'core area' has been cogently
demonstrated by Ernst Haas. His pioneering work has been reproduced in
Cosgrove & Twitchett, *New Internat. Actors*, pp. 76–92.

the European and the global policies of many of her leading European allies. Her condemnation of the Anglo-French Suez adventure of 1956 was perhaps more a dramatic rather than a unique example of the differences which arise on both sides of the Atlantic.

More significantly for the future, there is a wide divergence of economic interests. Douglas Jay among others has advocated a North Atlantic Free Trade Area as a better alternative for Britain than membership of the EEC.[63] But the NAFTA scheme is unattractive to the United States and there is insufficient community of economic interest to underpin such a scheme. Not only would Britain and the other Western European states probably be unable to compete with the economic power of the North American colossus, but a major impulse behind the movement for greater European co-operation is to make Western Europe a more viable economic entity in relation to the United States. The Kennedy Round negotiations demonstrated that the economic interests of the Six as a group are not synonymous with those of the United States. In the last few months there have been bitter exchanges between the Nixon Administration and the Commission of the European Communities: Washington dislikes the impact of the EEC's common agricultural policy on American farm exports while the Europeans resent the tariff structure of the United States. In view of the present uncertain economic outlook in the West generally, there could be some kind of trade war between the United States and Western Europe, particularly the EEC, in the near future.

The EEC is perhaps the only example of a true institutionalized community existing between states in the modern world. Although there are important differences among its members, they all place a high priority on its continuation and rarely, if ever, undertake external policies incompatible with Community membership. The EEC is underpinned by important interests in both the *Gemeinschaft* and the *Gesellschaft* senses. At the present time it seems highly improbable that other regional experiments will develop core areas resembling those found in the new Europe. But, at the end of the Second World War,

[63] *After the Common Market* (London, 1968).

few commentators foresaw either Franco-German rapprochement, let alone the emergence of the EEC.

Suggestions for Further Reading*

Bell, Coral. *The Asian balance of power: a comparison with European precedents*. London, ISS, 1968.

Buchan, Alastair. *A world of nuclear powers*. Englewood Cliffs, Prentice-Hall, 1966.

Collier, David S., & Kurt Glaser, eds. *The conditions for peace in Europe*. Washington, Public Affairs Press, 1969.

Frankel, Joseph. *National interest*. London, Pall Mall & Macmillan, 1970.

Garnett, John, ed. *Theories of peace and security: a reader in contemporary strategic thought*. London, Macmillan, 1970.

Herz, John H. *International politics in the atomic age*. New York, Columbia UP, 1959.

Hurewitz, J. C. *Middle East politics: the military dimension*. New York, Praeger, 1969.

Kahn, H. *On escalation*. London, Pall Mall, 1965.

Knorr, Klaus. *On the use of military power in the nuclear age*. Princeton UP, 1966.

Lyon, Peter. *Neutralism*. Leicester UP, 1963.

Maxwell, Stephen. *Rationality in deterrence*. London, ISS, 1968.

Schelling, Thomas C. *Arms and influence*. New Haven, Yale UP, 1966.

Waltz, Kenneth N. *Man, the state, and war*. New York, Columbia UP, 1959.

Young, Elizabeth. *The politics of non-proliferation: the 1968 treaty in hindsight and forecast*. London, ISS, 1969.

* Omitting works cited or referred to in the text.

2

TOWARDS A MORE DANGEROUS WORLD?

Neville Brown

I. The Super-Power Nuclear Balance

SINCE 1945 military science has undergone a cataclysmic change. Firepower used to be so scarce a resource that the supreme test of generalship lay in conserving it for application at the crucial time and place. Now it has become so abundant that men fear to use it save in the smallest fractions. Forty tons of artillery ammunition were expended at the Battle of Borodino—the main engagement during Napoleon's 1812 campaign against Russia; 50,000 tons were fired by the British artillery in the many days of bombardment that preceded the great Somme offensive of 1916. Perhaps 6 million tons were expended during the whole of the Second World War. Yet in the course of an all-out nuclear war the equivalent of some tens of thousands of millions of tons of TNT might well be exploded. Admittedly the extent of the destruction caused by large explosions (e.g. nuclear ones) is usually considerably less than might be expected from simple comparisons of energy yield. But to lay much stress on this would be to quibble. For this factor is far outweighed by the special nuclear phenomena of heat-flash and fall-out and by the possibility that, in a general war, the taboos which currently operate against microbiological weapons would be discarded. From this it follows that to the awesome impact of physical damage would be added numerous and extensive changes of a quite unprecedented kind—in the biological aspects of the human environment.

Already no fewer than five countries—the United States, the Soviet Union, Britain, China, and France—have attained or virtually attained thermonuclear status, by which is meant the ability independently to manufacture the exceptionally potent kind of nuclear warhead popularly known as the

' hydrogen bomb '. Likewise, a number of countries have for many years been engaged in research into at least the defensive side of microbiological warfare. Nevertheless, it almost certainly remains true to say that over 95 per cent of the destructive potential in the world is in the hands of the United States and the Soviet Union and has been accumulated principally as a result of the arms race between these two super-powers.

This arms race is a subject about which there is still a great deal of misunderstanding. Many people believe that ever since 1949—when the Soviet Union broke the United States nuclear monopoly—or perhaps since 1953—the year in which both powers acquired operational hydrogen bombs—a nuclear stalemate has existed between Washington and Moscow or, if one likes, between the Atlantic Alliance and what is now the Warsaw Pact. A different impression emerges, however, if consideration is given not just to the stockpiling of nuclear warheads but also to the means of delivery over, in particular, ' intercontinental ' ranges. An intercontinental weapon is understood as one which is capable of hitting the heart of the Soviet Union from the heart of the United States or vice versa.

For it is, in fact, only within the last year or so that the Soviet Union has drawn abreast of the United States at this all-important intercontinental level. As late as 1962 she lagged critically in this regard. Thus in June of that year the then Secretary of Defense, Robert McNamara, felt himself in a position to indicate, as he did in a speech at Ann Arbor in Michigan,[1] that for some time ahead the United States could expect to defeat the Soviet Union in any major conflict simply by means of attacks concentrated on ' all of the enemy's vital nuclear capabilities ', namely the launching pads of her Inter-Continental Ballistic Missiles (ICBMS). His confidence stemmed primarily from the way in which, using her new reconnaissance satellites, America had pinpointed all the Soviet Union's ICBMS and had shown them to be few in number, too large and complicated to fire at short notice, and lacking adequate ferro-concrete ' hardening ' against nuclear blast. The Soviet ICBM echelon was thereby shown to be vulnerable

[1] For the text of this speech see *Survival*, Sept. Oct. 1962, p. 194.

to complete, or almost complete, destruction on the ground in the event of a strategic rocket attack of the scale and precision the United States had become capable of launching. Some intercontinental bombers and missile-firing submarines might have survived, but these would not in themselves have been able to guarantee effective retaliation against the United States.

How is this recognition of a Total Counterforce option to be related to anxiety expressed in America in the middle 1950s about a ' bomber gap ' and in the late 1950s about a ' missile gap '? The appearance of two types of Soviet intercontinental bomber at the Tushino air display in 1955 demonstrated that the Russians had closed much of the gap that had existed between themselves and the West in 1945 in respect of the techniques of strategic bombing. The launching of Sputnik I in the autumn of 1957 indicated that they had the ability to fire a useful payload with considerable accuracy over, in particular, intercontinental distances. Why was neither advance exploited to effect a decisive numerical preponderance in regard to the strategic balance?

The answer can hardly be said to lie in any failure on the part of the Soviet Union to allocate sufficient resources to defence! But where a large part of it can be found is in the distribution of defence outlays. For here the rational criterion of relative cost-effectiveness has consistently been subordinated to other priorities. Usually the latter have been derived from military traditions that can, at least in some cases, be traced back to Tsarist times. Always they seem exceptionally well adapted to the provision of numerous posts for the large and influential Soviet officer corps.

One of the priorities in question has been the maintenance in western Russia of a large force of medium-range strategic bombers and—in this last decade—missiles: the aim being to pose an overwhelming deterrent against Central and Western Europe—the region from which nearly all the major threats Russia has had to cope with in the course of the last two centuries have emanated. Another has been an emphasis on the active air defence of the Soviet homeland so great as to appear totally unrealistic in an era in which, even if only a

few offensive warheads reach their targets, ma…
may die. For a couple of decades past there has be…
investment in the development and deployment o…
aircraft systems; and ever since 1960 or thereabouts A…
Ballistic missiles (ABMs) have been receiving much attention.
Indeed, it must be said that, in at least the first half of the
last decade, there was a marked contrast between the naive
enthusiasm displayed towards ABM systems in official circles
in Moscow and the astringent scepticism that still prevailed in
Washington.

But perhaps the most remarkable of the anomalies in the
Soviet effort has been the high proportion directed towards the
maintenance, on either an active or a reserve basis, of such
local war forces as mechanized and armoured divisions,
tactical air squadrons, and squadrons of warships. Had Soviet
military doctrine taken account of the possibility of extended
non-nuclear or limited nuclear war, this expenditure might
not have been unreasonable. However, her strategists have
always insisted that any major engagement involving the
West and herself would rapidly either cease or else ' go nuclear '
and, if the latter, swiftly become an all-out war. So what was the
use, for example, of the fleet of 600 or 700 submarines the Red
Navy built up during the 1950s? All of them had only conventional propulsion and armament. Moreover, most of them had
a relatively short range, a limitation made the more serious
by the land-locked and ice-locked character of the coastlines
from which they had to operate. The chief explanation adduced
by Soviet commentators at the time was that these vessels
would be used to intercept naval and merchant ships in the
North Atlantic in the event of general war. Yet surely it is
obvious that, in a general war fought in the all-out manner the
Russians themselves envisaged, the handicap the Western
alliance would have laboured under after the first one or two
hours would have been not a shortage of ships but a lack of
enough ports for them to proceed to. It is hard to avoid the
conclusion that the building of large numbers of submarines
was purely a matter of habit. Before 1914, and again before
1939, Russia had behaved in exactly the same way.

Attention has been drawn to the influence of this non-rational traditionalism because it may still be pervasive. Thus the Soviet attitude towards ABMs may be heavily conditioned by the simple thought that these defensive weapons are manifestly the best way to preserve the inviolability of the motherland. Then again, a continuation of the somewhat obsessive concern with deterrence against Europe is implied by the flight testing of a new swing-wing and supersonic medium-range strategic bomber and also by certain measures recently taken to strengthen the strategic-missile echelons opposite Western Europe. Even so, the 1962 crisis in Soviet deterrence cannot be explained solely in terms of the doctrinal conservatism of the Kremlin. Relevant also was the dynamism American science and technology was displaying in spite of the deep despondency about it shown by so many in the aftermath of Sputnik! From this dynamism came two break-throughs so rapid as to take not only the Russians completely by surprise.

The first of these was in reconnaissance from space. The reason why the Americans were able to pin-point all the Soviet ICBM sites was that, in the autumn of 1961, they had introduced unmanned orbiting satellites able to eject camera-film and so allow it to be collected at ground level, thereby avoiding the serious degradation of picture quality that reliance on wireless transmission would involve. Then, in April 1962, the first squadron of *Minuteman* solid-fuelled ICBMs started to enter service. The first generation of American ICBMs—the *Atlas* and the *Titan* 1—had, like their counterparts in the Soviet Union, been fuelled with 'unstorable' liquids, i.e. ones that could not be held for long inside an actual rocket. Therefore, each ICBM had to be supported by an elaborate complex of storage tanks and refrigeration equipment, which in its turn meant each missile silo was difficult to 'harden' with steel and concrete to an acceptable degree and also, of course, that overall procurement costs were high. Another weakness of the first-generation ICBMs was that it took a long time to prepare them for firing. This made synchronized release difficult and effectively ruled out their avoiding destruction on the ground by being launched after an incoming attack had been detected by radar.

But with the advent of the *Minuteman* the United States acquired a weapon system that could be hardened so effectively that about a dozen offensive rockets with single warheads had to be fired at any one of its sites to stand, let us say, a 90 per cent chance of destroying it. Furthermore, *Minuteman* is a weapon that can, if necessary, be fired at short notice and in accordance with quite an intricate salvoing plan. Above all, it is cheap. The overall installation cost of a *Minuteman* 2 has proved to be about $5 million. Running costs are of the order of $200,000 a year. The total American defence budget still exceeds $70,000 million a year.

By the autumn of 1962 the United States had 200 ICBMs in service and was emplacing extra *Minuteman* 1s at the rate of two every three days. Meanwhile, the Soviet Union had no more than 75 ICBMs operational and was expanding this force only slowly. Since then, however, this intercontinental balance has become a good deal more equal. By 1969 each of the superpowers had brought into service over 1,000 ICBMs, many of them fuelled either with a solid mixture or else with a storable liquid one, the latter having much the same advantages. Some years ago many hoped that a roughly symmetrical balance would prove the basis for a prolonged period of stability in the relationship of mutual deterrence between Russia and America, a stability that would encourage the evolution of more relaxed attitudes in other spheres.

Yet already anxiety is widespread about the apparent imminence of a major intensification of this strategic arms race, primarily in response to technological innovation. Multiple Independently Targetable Re-entry Vehicles (MIRVs) have lately been brought to a remarkably high degree of perfection. Meanwhile, some concern is being expressed about allegedly dramatic breakthroughs, actual or impending, in the means of locating ballistic missile submarines.[2] The work being done on ABMs and certain other strategic systems adds to the sense of flux.

The principle of the MIRV is that, as the warhead capsule of an offensive rocket descends to its target area, a supplementary booster within it sends out several thermonuclear warheads all on different vectors. In 1968 the United States test-fired two systems which could incorporate MIRVs, one being the *Poseidon*

[2] See the author's ' Deterrence from the Sea ', *Survival*, June 1970, pp. 194–8.

submarine-launched rocket and the other the *Minuteman* 3
ICBM. At about the same time MIRVs were released in launches
across the Pacific range of the Soviet ss–9 ICBM. Three warheads
with an estimated yield of five megatons apiece were ejected
from each ss–9 capsule; these then descended in patterns that
suggested an ability to hit a group of three *Minuteman* sites
with standard accuracies so high that all the sites in question
would most probably either be wrecked or smothered in crater
debris.

Analysts have concluded that the 500 emplaced ss–9s predicted
for 1976 or thereabouts could destroy in one blow 95 per cent
of the 1,000 *Minuteman* 2s and 3s the United States is scheduled
to have by then.[3] Therefore, or so the argument runs, unless
the Russians can be persuaded to halt ss–9 deployment, the
United States will have to move rapidly ahead with an ABM
point defence of her hardened ICBM sites in order to introduce
another major uncertainty into calculations about the feasibility
of surprise attack. What makes this appreciation the more
disturbing is that it rests on an estimate for the ss–9 build-up
that may well turn out to be too conservative. Towards the end
of the 1970s the Soviet ICBM echelon included 240 ss–9s.[4]

But is the overall situation really as alarming as this assessment
appears to imply? Were, say, a mere 50 *Minutemen* to survive
a Soviet first-strike they could dispatch warheads with yields
in the megaton range against about 100 Soviet urban targets
—that is, against the home neighbourhoods of perhaps 40–50
million people. Besides, the static ICBM is by no means the only
instrument of strategic retaliation available. More than 300
B–52 and FB–111 bombers will remain in service with Strategic
Air Command through the early 1970s, and their ability to
reach well-defended targets, though indeterminate, may well
not be negligible. By the same token, although microbiological
warfare is usually neglected in discussions of the central arms
balance, it should not be thought irrelevant to it. Suppose one
side had lost all its ICBMs and yet had been able to preserve, by
means of dispersion, part of its bomber fleet: it is quite conceivable that a significant threat of total annihilation could still be

[3] Albert Wohlstetter, ' Defence in the 1970s ', ibid. Aug. 1969, pp. 242–5.
[4] ISS, *Military Balance, 1970–1.*

maintained by equipping those bombers with biological weapons.

Where the crux of the matter lies, however, is in the reliance both super-powers will be placing on sea-based deterrence in the years immediately ahead. The United States commissioned her first ballistic-missile submarine in 1960. Now she has in service 41 nuclear-driven Fleet Ballistic-Missile submarines, each with 16 *Polaris* missiles: no fewer than 31 of these FBMS will eventually incorporate various mixes of MIRVS and decoys, thanks to the replacement of *Polaris* by *Poseidon*. By 1969 the corresponding Soviet fleet also consisted of about 40 vessels, nearly half being nuclear driven. Nevertheless, this force carried a mere 150 strategic rockets, all with ranges below 1,000 miles. But over the last year or so a new type of Soviet ballistic submarine has been observed; and each member of this Y-class is equipped with 16 missiles with a payload and range performance apparently very similar to that of *Polaris*. Presumably these missiles, too, can be adapted to carry multiple warheads and other penetration aids. From now on units of the Y-class will be joining the Red Navy at a rate of something like six to eight a year.

The notion that ballistic-missile submarines are about to be compromised by vastly improved detection methods partly rests on accounts of the use of infra-red sensors mounted in unmanned orbiting satellites to detect the small rise in the temperature of the sea surface that the passage of a submerged submarine may occasion, chiefly because of the heat generated by its own propulsion units. However, a number of elementary yet fundamental questions spring immediately to mind. What if the vessel is moving only slowly and at great depth? What about cloud cover? Suppose the submarine glides beneath some ice? What if a heavy sea is running? How well can the sensors discriminate against reflected sunlight and other spurious sources? What can be done about positive identification? How long does data of this sort take to transmit and interpret? Certain of these doubts are accentuated by reports that, although requirements in this sphere are less exact than those for anti-submarine warfare, meteorological satellites have some difficulty in obtaining satisfactory readings of surface temperature.[5]

[5] *New Scientist*, 2 Oct. 1969.

So it is very hard to believe that this technique could ever have more than an auxiliary value in anti-submarine surveillance. Likewise it is most improbable that progress in other means of location will render such vessels as the FBMS obsolete. Admittedly reference has often been made to the advances made in acoustic detection in recent years. As often as not, however, the discussion takes the form of a comparison with the situation towards the end of the Battle of the Atlantic,[6] whereas the setting for strategic war would be one more conducive to the survival of the submarine. This is because a ballistic-missile submarine is concerned not with tracking enemy vessels but with eluding them, in which aim it is assisted by an ability to cruise quietly and fully submerged for perhaps two months on end. Besides, even in May 1943—a month of decisive victory for the escort forces in the Battle of the Atlantic—the average attrition of U-Boats at sea was a bare 1·0 per cent per day:[7] anti-submarine forces would have to do much better than that in order to play a useful part in any thermonuclear conflict.

In the light of these realities, many of the technical improvements registered during the last two decades look insufficient. Such is undoubtedly the case, for example, in regard to acoustic sensoring. Active sonar sets mounted in submerged submarines can occasionally recapture pulses that have bounced off targets well over fifty miles away. Standard passive-sensoring equipment can sometimes pick up emissions from moving submarines across 100 miles or more. Ranges of several hundred miles have been registered experimentally with exceptionally large sonar transducers located in big surface ships. But all these distances are puny in proportion to the total extent of the oceans and do not, in any case, represent norms. Mechanical and biological sea noise will often cause serious interference. Sound waves will be extensively refracted and reflected by the many changes, both gradual and abrupt, that occur in the temperature and salinity of sea water, especially in the vertical plane.

Besides, any further significant advances in the detection of fully submerged submarines will be extremely hard to make.

---

[6] For instance, Sir Peter Gretton, *Maritime Strategy* (London, 1965), p. 116.

[7] Sir Arthur Hezlet, *The Submarine and Sea-Power* (London, 1967), p. 183.

Thus, the geometry of the movement of sound as a form of radiant energy is such that, for any given output, the recorded strength of a reflected pulse will always be inversely proportional to the fourth power of the range being achieved, i.e. if the range is doubled the echo received will diminish by 15/16ths. Furthermore, acoustic energy is readily absorbed by sea water. Low-frequency sound waves are, of course, attenuated less than high-frequency ones but are also much more difficult to generate, are more susceptible to background noise, and are less suitable for target discrimination. Objections that are similar, and far more serious, can be levelled against any application of electromagnetic-wave motion to this end.

To say all this is not to imply that submarines are without any drawbacks when cast in the role of strategic-delivery platforms. Total installation costs tend to be something like three times as much per missile as is the case with *Minuteman*—a differential which though by no means decisive, is bound to figure in any debate about priorities. Furthermore, command and control is sometimes more difficult in the case of the submarines. Herein lies one reason why submarines would not be suitable for active participation in the limited or slow-motion strategic wars that both Soviet and American theorists believe could break out under certain circumstances. Another is that if, say, an FBM fires a single missile, it automatically betrays the position of another fifteen. The implication is that absolute dependence on ballistic submarines could never be appropriate for deterrent strategies as universal and multilateral as those of the super-powers.

Moreover, by 1980 or thereabouts mobile ICBMs are quite likely to be entering service; and this innovation should be able to offer, within one class of weapon, a unique combination of flexibility and stability. But in the meantime, it is in the existence of weapons like *Polaris* and *Poseidon* that the best hope lies of preventing MIRVs from wrecking the nuclear deadlock between the super-powers.

What then of the ABM, the weapon that seems about to become the key defensive element in the spectrum of strategic deterrence? Very swift advances in computer design and other branches of electronics will enable some of the main ABM components to become ever more refined. All the same, there are two major unknowns in the field of ABM performance. One is the exact effect nuclear explosions in or near the ionized layers of the upper atmosphere can have on ground-based radar and how this may best be minimized. The other is the kill radii of ABM warheads at high altitudes: how great these are and whether the critical factor is blast, gamma-radiation, or neutron flux. Only a limited number of high altitude nuclear explosions had been carried out when further ones were precluded, so far as signatories were concerned, by the partial test ban of 1963, i.e. the treaty banning nuclear-weapons tests in the atmosphere, outer space, and the oceans.

What makes this collective restraint so significant is the fact that the highly peculiar properties of the atmosphere several tens of miles above the surface cannot be simulated in anything like a perfect way close to the ground. Therefore, so long as the 1963 treaty is honoured, nobody will be at all sure what level of efficiency ABMS are capable of or how this is to be attained. What then are the strategic implications? Might not all the uncertainties that surround ABM performance be an extra source of stability? For could any prospective aggressor afford to risk a surprise attack if both he and his adversary had come to rely heavily on ABMS?

Official circles in the United States do, in fact, contend that the installation of ABMS to shield the *Minuteman* hard sites, as per the 1969 *Safeguard* revision of the ABM programme, will constitute a stabilizing, as well as an economical, exploitation of technological uncertainty to deter any MIRV attack the Russians may contemplate.[8] Even so, once ICBM hard sites have been thus protected, it might be thought only prudent to extend some coverage, at least against random or accidental attack, to such nodal military objectives as the home bases of the FBMS or some of the big command centres ashore.[9] Vital research establishments might come next. Once these had been brought under the

[8] Statement by Secretary of Defense Melvin Laird to the House of Representatives Committee on Appropriations, Subcommittee on Department of Defense Appropriations, 25 Feb. 1970.

[9] Even the present plans provide for ABM protection for the National Command Authority in Washington D.C.

Safeguard umbrella, the United States would be well on the way to general ABM deployment.

To envisage this progression in its entirety may well be to look something of the order of ten to twelve years ahead. A likelihood to reckon with, however, is that the perceived threat from China will soon give a powerful additional impetus to any trend towards area deployment. The key to the correlation here being made is as follows. Point defence is a counter-Soviet move because it is confidently assumed that, in any case, the first generation Chinese rockets will not be accurate enough to threaten such objectives as hardened missile sites. Conversely, the defence of broad areas of human settlement could be rational only as a counter-Chinese measure, it being generally conceded that, in the event of a heavy and sophisticated Soviet onslaught, it would be impossible to achieve the very high degree of effectiveness needed to make the whole endeavour worthwhile.

So when, in the autumn of 1967, Robert McNamara announced that the United States intended to ' go ahead with a limited ABM deployment ', he said this programme—which had been named *Sentinel*—was intended to give a ' thin-screen ' defence of American cities against the sort of intercontinental threat the Chinese might be posing in the mid-1970s.[10] Likewise, though the explicit immediate purpose of the *Safeguard* modification of *Sentinel* outlined by Richard Nixon on 14 March 1969 was the protection of *Minuteman*, the new President did make it clear that eventual area deployment against a possible Chinese attack had by no means been excluded,[11] and since then, indeed, this interest in deterring Peking appears to have increased.[12]

Although the installation of ABMs the Soviet Union began in 1966 has been proceeding only slowly, it is already apparent that so far she has seen this weapon chiefly as a way to minimize the effects of a pre-emptive or retaliatory strike against Russian towns and cities by moderate numbers of relatively unsophisticated offensive rockets. Everything that is known about the

[10] ' Address to Editors and Publishers of United Press International, San Francisco, 18 September 1967 ', *Documents on American Foreign Relations 1967*, pp. 65–81.

[11] For the text see *Survival*, May 1969, pp. 146–8.

[12] George Rathjens ' ABM Defence Against China ', ibid., July 1970, pp. 225–6, see also Melvin Laird's statement (n. 8 above).

characteristics of the *Galosh* ABM system supports this interpretation. So does the priority accorded the Moscow district in the initial deployment. Nor need we be surprised. For this preoccupation is very much in accord with the traditional bias in favour of the comprehensive defence of the homeland.

What must be acknowledged, on the other hand, is that the distribution of *Galosh* batteries around Moscow has not been such as to suggest any particular concern with China, although she is the one potential adversary against whom ABM area defence might stand some chance of being sufficiently effective. All the same, this situation is one that could well change as China's own capability develops. One reason for saying this is that the first generation Chinese deterrent, being land-based and immobile, will be just as vulnerable to a Total Counterforce attack as was the Soviet deterrent in 1962. Therefore, Peking may feel obliged to rely for deterrence on the threat of a ' pre-emptive strike ' (i.e. a forestalling blow), with all the attendant risks of war through miscalculation. Rather than live under the shadow of this menace, however, the Soviet Union may prepare to thwart any such pre-emption by means of ABMs.

The objections to comprehensive ABM deployment by either super-power have been enumerated so often that there is now a danger that sheer familiarity will undermine their impact. Even so, their intrinsic merits remain as strong as ever. For substantial economic and enormous social strains could be generated by the continuous innovation of a whole variety of advanced defensive and offensive systems a full-scale ABM deployment could lead on to. Strategic bombers or cruise-missiles might enjoy a new lease of life by virtue of being able to underfly ABM defences; this resurgence could, in its turn, induce vast outlays on new surface-to-air systems specifically designed to combat them. Then again, what could be presented as a logical necessity to keep potentially hostile submarines at such a distance from coastal cities as to facilitate the safe interception of any rockets they discharge could well compromise hopelessly the free navigation of the high seas in time of peace—a principle which, ironically enough, both the United States and the Soviet Union have often been keen to uphold. A more direct hazard is that eventually even the partial test ban will fall victim to an endless drive for esoteric refinement within the ABM field itself. True the inhibitions against its abrogation look strong at the moment. But these might weaken rapidly in the tense atmosphere of a new arms race.

To draw attention to the more sombre possibilities is not to discount any hope of tangible progress being made in the Strategic Arms Limitation Talks (SALT) between the Soviet Union and the United States that began in Helsinki in November 1969 and were resumed in Vienna in April 1970. But it would be quite wrong to allow the pursuit of stability in the arms balance between the super-powers to become completely dependent on the outcome of these exchanges. For there are at least two good reasons why the governments in question should be urged to exercise restraint, whether any formal or tacit agreements are reached in the SALT talks or not. One is that prior restraint will make it easier to arrive at any such under-standings. The other is that a satisfactory accord may, in any case, be far from easy to obtain at the SALT discussions. Why should this particular forum yield more positive results than all the informal conversations about strategic deterrence Moscow and Washington have held over the last few years? Does it not labour under similar handicaps?

One fundamental obstacle is the difference in political culture and military tradition between the two sides. Related to it is the continuing prevalence of 'hawkishness', especially within the respective military hierarchies. Thus in recent years various elements within the Soviet armed forces appear to have played a significant part in keeping their government committed to the overall aim of 'military superiority' as opposed to mere 'parity'.[13] It is notable that the Soviet military leadership did nothing to prevent the overthrow of Premier Khrushchev in 1964, although it had done much to facilitate his triumph over the 'anti-Party group' in 1957.[14] Then again, a total collapse of United States policy in Indochina could easily

[13] See Thomas W. Wolfe, 'Soviet Military Policy', *Survival*, Jan. 1968, pp. 2–27, and Malcolm Mackintosh, 'Soviet Strategic Policy', *World Today*, July 1970, pp. 269–76.
[14] See C. A. Linden, *Khrushchev and the Soviet Leadership 1957–64* (Baltimore, 1966), p. 205. See also Victor Zorza, *Life*, 16 Nov. 1964, and Gabriel Lorince, *New Statesman*, 2 May 1969.

cause a strong surge of opinion in that country away from global involvement and towards ' Fortress America ', the shift being symbolized by a switch of defence priorities from local war to strategic forces. Moreover, it is not too hard to demonstrate arithmetically that, even if this were associated with a sharp contraction of total military outlays, the end-result would almost certainly be an increase of expenditure on new strategic weapons.

Another vexatious matter concerns the extent to which the SALT talks can, and should, embrace political matters. For instance, must not any examination of the possibility of an ABM freeze include some evaluation of China's long-term intentions? Few would deny that, within a few years, Peking ought to be able to confront her potential adversaries with a substantial offensive threat. So the key point at issue is whether she will use this for genuine deterrence or for more belligerent aims. Unfortunately, however, extensive Soviet-American exchanges, under the auspices of the SALT talks, about China's ultimate motives might well increase her sense of isolation. They would also tend to lead on to a dialogue about the general political scene. Yet were this evolution to take place, the accent on arms control would be weakened, basic disagreements about such chronic trouble spots as the Middle East might be highlighted, and each country's allies might become restive and suspicious.

Another crucial problem is that of arms-control surveillance. An integral, and very important, part of Russia's traditional preoccupation with territorial inviolability is her deep concern for national privacy. Thus she is till loath to release anything other than a minimal amount of information about the size and configuration of her military establishment. Furthermore, she remains adamantly opposed to any international ' on-site ' inspections of suspected nuclear tests or nuclear reactors or any similar phenomena or facilities within her own boundaries. Sometimes she has been reluctant even to acknowledge explicitly that overflights by U-2 manned aircraft (between 1956 and 1960) or by ' spy satellites ' (since 1961) have given the West exact answers to quite a number of salient questions.[15] Likewise, she

[15] Reconnaissance satellites are now quite capable of detecting vehicles moving along roads.

has persistently treated as highly confidential much that is, in fact, readily observable by this method. Herein lies another reason why, though the SALT discussions may produce some tacit understandings, they are unlikely to yield blueprints for disarmament.

Nor is it just the Soviet Union that is prone to be acutely sensitive about being regularly reconnoitred from space. Many of the 135 states in the contemporary world are, by Western standards, ' closed societies ' and therefore unlikely to welcome general dissemination of the sort of information about themselves satellites can gather. So what should the United States, in particular, do with all the data it is collecting? To release select portions of it would be to expose itself to charges of news manipulation; and, indeed, such accusations have already been levelled in regard to the surveillance of the Soviet Union. To disseminate it on a confidential basis—e.g. to university geography departments!—would be to appear guilty of a new form of patronage. Yet to make it freely available would be to arouse even more widespread antagonism. The dilemmas of choice here posed are bound to be accentuated by continuous advances in the relevant techniques. For these could well lead to the introduction of much bigger reconnaissance satellites or space platforms with large telescopic lenses and other advanced forms of equipment.

II. The Diffused Accumulation of Plutonium

Surveillance is by no means the only sphere in which scientific progress is liable to generate strains between the emerging nations and the more developed ones. The fabrication of weapons is certainly another. Here the essential point is that the ability to maintain sophisticated military establishments is extending ever more widely through the world at large, chiefly as a natural consequence of economic and social progress. How far emerging nations will exploit this trend to amass ever more armed strength will depend upon a whole variety of factors.[16] Among them

[16] Between 1958 and 1969 annual defence expenditure, at 1960 prices, is estimated to have risen from $9,600,000,000 to $22,200,000,000 in the world, excluding NATO and the Warsaw Pact. See Stockholm International Peace Research Inst., *Yearbook of World Armaments and Disarmament, 1969/70*, pt. 2, table 1a, p. 267.

will be the extent to which the more advanced states limit their own military ambitions. If, in particular, the two super-powers began to deploy MIRVS or ABMS extensively in a mutual but competitive quest for ' military superiority ' or ' comprehensive defence ', the prospects for general arms limitation—either formal or tacit—would thereby be substantially diminished.

The need for exemplary restraint becomes especially evident in the light of the Treaty on the Non-Proliferation of Nuclear Weapons (NPT), under which signatories pledge themselves to halt the spread of nuclear weapons and, more specifically, the non-nuclear nations agree to accept inspection ' . . . in accordance with the statute of the International Atomic Energy Agency and the Agency's safeguards system ' (Art. III).[17] The NPT was opened for signature on 1 July 1968. Among the emergent or potential nuclear powers that had not acceded by July 1970 were Argentina, Brazil, China, France, India, Indonesia, Israel, Pakistan, and South Africa. All have had their own special reasons for delay but most have also been influenced by a general feeling that, at least in its present form, the NPT discriminates too heavily in favour of the existing nuclear powers. Thus India has categorically stated that, for this very reason, she will not sign the treaty as it now stands. Meanwhile, China and France have consistently refused even to negotiate about any arms-control possibilities that would, in their view, merely crystallize a super-power hegemony. The attempts to work out the details of the surveillance called for in Article III might well exacerbate this anxiety about discrimination.

Furthermore, the NPT does not bind irrevocably those who do accede to it. Any party can withdraw at no more than three months' notice should it decide 'that extraordinary events, related to the subject-matter of this Treaty, have jeopardized the supreme interests of its country ' (Art. X). The text of the treaty also stresses that all signatories have the right to expect it to lead to genuine progress towards general and complete disarmament. Nothing would induce more cynicism on this score than widespread ABM or MIRV deployment on the part of the United States and the Soviet Union.

[17] For full text see UN, *Treaty on the Non-Proliferation of Nuclear Weapons* (New York, 1969).

Scientific and industrial change is making this question of ' horizontal ' nuclear proliferation more urgent than ever before. One aspect is the research under way in various countries on the ' enrichment ' of natural uranium by means of the gas centrifuge. By ' enrichment ' is meant increasing the proportion of the relatively fissile isotope, Uranium 235, so as to facilitate either a controlled chain-reaction inside a nuclear reactor or— if the sample in question is enriched to 90 per cent or so—to render possible a reaction of a more explosive kind. The problem is that, since the chemical behaviour of all the isotopes of the same element is identical, these isotopes cannot be separated by chemical means. The solution initially adopted by all the existing thermonuclear states—namely, Britain, China, France, the Soviet Union, and the United States—was ' gaseous diffusion ', which involves exploiting the differences in atomic weights between the respective isotopes by constantly passing gasified uranium through porous barriers. But gaseous diffusion requires very high quality technology and large-scale operation: the centrifugal technique should be more easily within reach of the smaller industrial states. Most probably, for example, it holds the key to South Africa's claim, made in July 1970, that she has found a means of uranium enrichment.

No less pertinent is the vast expansion now imminent in the use of nuclear energy for civil purposes. Here the crux of the matter is that, in the course of the production of heat and power by the consumption of natural or enriched uranium, another fissile material—Plutonium 239—is formed; and this artificial isotope can readily be distinguished by chemical means from the rest of the sludge in which it accumulates. Moreover, although even its long-term industrial value appears only limited, it is eminently suitable for the fabrication of nuclear warheads. A bomb of the same strength as, say, the 20-kiloton one dropped over Nagasaki requires only about 5 kilogrammes. As much would normally be created each year by the continuous generation of between 10 and 20 megawatts (MW) of electricity.[18]

Improvements in coal- and oil-fired power stations have

[18] Early expectations that, as a rule, the Plutonium 239 obtained from power reactors would be satisfactorily contaminated by another isotope, Plutonium 240, have more recently been discounted. See Leonard Beaton, *Must the Bomb Spread?* (1966), pp. 97–8 and *Military Balance 1970–1*, p. 125.

lately been sufficiently marked to prevent the industrial application of nuclear energy proceeding as rapidly as was generally expected some twelve to fifteen years ago. Nevertheless, all the indications are that, from now on, nuclear power stations with a generating capacity of 500 MW or more will normally be competitive with their conventional counterparts. Another safe prediction is that nuclear plants of several times the first-mentioned size will soon be built, thereby realizing additional economies of scale of a considerable magnitude. True the fact that few conventional power stations are larger than 300 MW suggests that the capacities just mentioned will usually be in excess of local requirements, especially in the developing regions. Even in the third world, however, it will occasionally be possible to justify economically the construction of ultra-large establishments, e.g. for desalination, irrigation, or the mass production of fertilizer.[19] Two other simple truths should also be remembered. One is that the ' break-even ' point between conventional and nuclear power stations is likely to fall gradually. The other is that, for a variety of reasons, the tendency will be to adopt the nuclear solution even though it may not be the best in terms of comparative cost.

Besides, these energy-producing installations are by no means the only factor in this equation. To them must be added the research reactors. Already several hundred of these units are dotted round some fifty countries and many of them have a significant net yield of plutonium. Perhaps the most important, at least from the strategic point of view, is the natural uranium facility at Dimona in Israel. Dimona's capacity is rated at 24 thermal MW which, for our present purposes, can be taken as equivalent to 7 or 8 MW of transmitted electricity.[20] But most of the other research reactors are a good deal smaller. To some extent too, the problem they pose is limited by many being located within the national boundaries of the five present members of the military ' nuclear club '. Even so, it is still significant.

By early 1969 the total nuclear megawattage in the world had only reached a modest 20,000, as against 6,100 in 1964 and

[19] Dr Sanat Biswas, ' India's Nuclear Dawn ', *New Scientist*, 10 July 1969, pp. 59–61.

[20] Beaton, *Must the Bomb Spread?*, p. 78.

1,400 in 1959. Nevertheless, if certain authoritative forecasts turn out to be correct, at least 150,000 MW will have been installed in the United States alone by 1980. West Germany is expected to have 4,500 MW by 1975 and 25,000 by 1980; the other founder members of the EEC should have rather more between them on the latter date. Japan should have almost as much as Federal Germany. Britain's installed capacity, too, should be of the same order.[21]

As has already been implied, however, economic circumstances throughout most of Africa, Asia, and Latin America will not favour so rapid a diffusion of capacity. Overall energy requirements will remain lower and, in many cases, the high cost of transmission, especially over distances of several hundred miles, will tend to favour a pattern of small, and therefore conventional, power stations. The fact that, for these and other reasons, nuclear energy will remain economically more marginal in the ' third world ' helps make the rate of its spread there hard to predict at all accurately. Another imponderable is the extent to which newly emerging nations will be attracted to nuclear energy because it is prestigious and, indeed, because it does proffer a measure of strategic independence. Yet despite these uncertainties, some projections can now be made. India is likely to have, however, six reactors with a combined capacity of over 1,000 MW by 1975. Pakistan will then have 350 MW. Among the other Asian countries with capacities in excess of 100 MW will be Israel, Taiwan, and, of course, Japan.[22]

From statistics such as these it can be deduced that civil reactors will be making enough plutonium every year by 1980 to provide the fissile cores for something like 10,000 extra nuclear warheads! Even if the existing members of the ' nuclear club ' are excluded, a total of several thousand is arrived at. Admittedly much of this latter capacity will be found either in Western Europe (excluding Britain and France) or else in Japan, but a fraction will be spread more widely; and, from the strategic point of view, this fraction can by no means be discounted. After all, the form of firepower under discussion is so terrible that even miniscule proportions could have horrific

[21] C. F. Barnaby & others, *The Nuclear Future* (London, June 1969), pp. 2–3.
[22] Ibid., Table 2.

consequences. Dimona may rank as a small reactor but Israel is accumulating enough nuclear material there to make a Nagasaki bomb almost every year. Even the relatively tiny Soviet-built research reactor the Yugoslavs have operated since 1959 can yield sufficient for two such warheads every decade. And, although a nuclear device of Nagasaki size would now be described as ' low-yield tactical ', it would be able to damage beyond repair virtually all brick buildings within a radius of a mile or more.

It is difficult to imagine the diffused accumulation of plutonium being adequately controlled without this waste material being purchased and disposed of by the International Atomic Energy Agency (IAEA) or some other external authority. Yet the NPT makes no provision for such purchase and disposal; nor do any of the safeguard agreements operative today. Among the latter are certain bilateral and regional ones and some under IAEA auspices. All that they do is watch the various stages in the importation and consumption of natural and enriched uranium so as to guarantee the honouring of contractual pledges not to exploit the programmes in question for military ends. The Plutonium 239 thereby formed remains in the hands of the user state.

But who can suppose that inspection routines that, in the nature of things, could not always be credibly supported by sanctions could ensure that no state would ever go back on its word and divert plutonium to ulterior purposes? Solemn international commitments have often been disregarded as circumstances have altered. And the temptation to employ military stocks of plutonium that were growing the whole time, and which were not being subject to reduction by commercial use,[23] could easily become greater than some countries could withstand.

Nor is this pure speculation. India has already provided a disturbing indication of the kind of turn events may take. The fact that she promised Canada that she would not use her

---

[23] It is generally expected that, by the 1980s, ' fast breeder reactors' will be in service, using as fuel a mixture of plutonium and uranium. As their name implies, however, these reactors are designed to produce more Plutonium 239 than they consume. No plans appear to exist for reactors fuelled entirely by plutonium.

original reactor to make 'the bomb' did not stop some of her leading spokesmen, including Pandit Nehru, from claiming forthwith that their country now had a nuclear option. Nor did it inhibit her from giving high priority to the construction of a plutonium separation plant, using the singularly unconvincing pretext that this was needed to provide fuel for the next generation of civil reactors.[24] Here the contention is not that India has yet come at all close to crossing the military nuclear threshold: it is that she has not regarded such a move as inconceivable. Anxiety on this score has not been diminished by the speed with which the launching of China's first space satellite was followed by the announcement of an expansion of India's nuclear and space programmes.[25]

A possibility that adds an extra dimension to the proliferation threat is that certain nations without the skill or resources to build nuclear weapons might make some cheap and simple arrangements for 'bee-sting' retaliation in chemical or micro-biological form. For both these methods of mass destruction lend themselves to comparatively small-scale and unsophisticated development and fabrication.

All this suggests that the belief of President Eisenhower and others in the 1950s that the nuclear age could be redeemed by what he called 'atoms for peace' may have been too sanguine. As is often emphasized, however, an ability to acquire military nuclear status is by no means always associated with a will to do so. Thus it can convincingly be argued that if in, say, 1960 all the countries concerned had decided to develop 'the bomb' as fast as possible, the present membership of the 'nuclear club' would be not five but a dozen.

III. Economic and Demographic Pressures

But can it be taken for granted that as much restraint will be manifest through the 1970s and beyond? Perhaps complacency on this score has been buttressed by a convention that is all too well established in the analysis of international problems—the almost invariable separation of studies of military security from those of economic and social development.

[24] Beaton, *Must the Bomb Spread?* pp. 57-8 & 72-3.
[25] *The Times*, 27 May 1970.

Not that the reasons are hard to identify, for the very impulses that induce humanitarians and liberals to take an interest in development tend also to inhibit them from any systematic consideration of the techniques of war. Soldiers, on the other hand, characteristically depend for their motivation on loyalty towards whomsoever they have sworn allegiance, a sentiment which may sometimes be sustained by rather simplistic and lopsided notions about the origins of particular conflicts. A similar, though usually less pronounced, orientation is to be observed in civilian government. It may be pertinent to add that, whereas the economic and social reformers generally think long-term, those concerned with the avoidance or resolution of armed conflict must frequently think short-term: a difference in perspective which helps to perpetuate the more basic cleavage.

Perhaps some would claim that full weight is now being given to economics and sociology in what is still the most intense international conflict in progress, namely the counter-insurgency campaign in Vietnam. But whether this is so is open to debate. What might be argued is that the Vietnam war might not have been so bitter or prolonged if, ten or twelve years ago, adequate attention had been given to land reform, government institutions, or agricultural techniques. Nor is it just in regard to the third world that this neglect of economic and social factors is to be observed. How often do strategists consider the likely geopolitical effects of social change within the Eastern European countries or, for that matter, in the advanced industrial nations of the North Atlantic area? Must not the steady progress towards affluence in Eastern Europe eventually influence the balance of power? Has not the student revolt in the West strategic implications? Is not the external policy of any country intimately related to its internal situation?

The truth is that strategic studies evolved as a separate discipline principally in order to assist those who operate in the defence and diplomatic fields. Therefore, it has tended to share their preoccupation with deterrence and with military and political crises. Perhaps India may once more be cited, affording as she does a good illustration of the imbalance thereby created. Strategists often ask themselves what would be the significance of India making 'the bomb'. Yet they rarely consider the possible consequences of her suffering an economic collapse or of the secession of some states or regions, contingencies which might have even more far-reaching strategic consequences.

In popular discussion, often it is said that the prime threat to mankind now comes not from the nuclear bomb but from the population explosion. Yet surely little thought is required to perceive that these are but different facets of the general problem of violence. For might not an excessive pressure of population on resources help to induce nuclear irresponsibility, and might not nuclear warheads be added to the familiar assortment of clumsy and macabre Malthusian checks?

Naturally many people found Secretary of State Dean Rusk's anxiety about the prospect of ' a billion Chinese on the mainland armed with nuclear weapons ' too reminiscent of the ' Yellow Peril' phobias of the turn of the century.[26] But in more general terms the combinations of manpower and firepower that are becoming possible are entirely legitimate subjects for concern. A nuclear war could yet prove to be the manner in which our species, or some large portion of it, effects a ' population crash' comparable to the ones which, according to the zoologists, have sometimes terminated phases of rapid population growth in other parts of the animal kingdom.[27]

Nor should attention be confined to a possible morbid connection between economic underdevelopment and the quest for weapons of mass destruction. For some correlations of this kind can already be established in the sub-nuclear forms of armed violence. Admittedly it is hard to find instances in the twentieth century of a genuine competition for ' living space ' being a prime cause of major conflict, the *lebensraum* theories formulated by certain fascist regimes in the 1930s having borne little relation to any real migratory need. But this does not mean that Dean Rusk was wrong when he gave warning that this situation could change by the 1980s if the population explosion

[26] Press Conference Washington, 12 Oct. 1967 (*New York Times*, 13 Oct. 1967).

[27] H. G. Andrewartha, ' Population Growth and Control: Animal Populations ', in Anthony Allison, *Population Control* (Pelican, 1970).

F

is not successfully tackled.[28] Even today it is possible to identify conflict situations in which land hunger plays a part. The bitter border dispute (known as ' the football war ') associated with the settlement in 1969 in Honduras of a quarter of a million Salvadoreans could be seen in part as the product of a struggle for living space on the part of El Salvador, the most densely populated country on the American continent.[29] Palestinian pressure for a ' right of return ' is one of the central factors in the Arab-Israel conflict. Extensive emigration by the Ibos from their desperately overcrowded heartland in the Eastern Region of Nigeria laid the basis for the communal tensions that led eventually to the Nigerian civil war. Then again, the armed strife within Indonesia between 1956 and 1961 clearly owed something to demographic imbalance. According to the 1962 census, 36 million people then lived on the 50,000 square miles of Java and Madura but only 37 million on the 700,000 square miles that make up the rest of the archipelago.

Of more immediate concern may be the general propensity of governments that feel insecure on the domestic front to ' export tension ' by resorting to aggressive external postures. Sukarno's Indonesia has often been taken as a case study of this process, which may have contributed materially to other confrontations that have occurred in Africa and Asia since 1945.[30]

Naturally, other factors besides economic and social ones also contribute to instability. Let us take, for example, the spate of guerrilla campaigns that has occurred since 1945. It is notable that several of the most serious (e.g. China, Greece, Malaya, Philippines, and Vietnam) have taken place in territories which were overrun in the Second World War. Part of the explanation is that the melancholy sequence of occupation, resistance, and liberation often meant that unofficial groups acquired abnormally free access to arms supplies, and in most cases these were hoarded for later use.

While members of the ' New Left ' may cherish a romantic stereotype of the guerrilla spiriting all the weapons he needs

[28] *The Times*, 12 Jan. 1968.

[29] ISS, *Strategic Survey 1969*, pp. 55-60.

[30] See, for example, Patrick Honey, *Communism in North Vietnam* (Cambridge, Mass., 1963). He stresses the part tension in the North played in the revival of the Vietnam conflict.

away from government forces, experience shows that the full complement of arms and—above all—the stocks of ammunition needed for final victory are hard to obtain without some external source of supply. As much was demonstrated by the course of the Greek civil war between 1946 and 1949. What had been a formidable Communist insurgency collapsed rapidly after Yugoslavia ceased to render active assistance, following her expulsion from the Cominform in 1948. Moreover, it is safe to assume that had the geography of the border not been so favourable to forms of indirect aggression as practical as arms smuggling, the fighting in Greece would never have become as extensive as it did.

Other aspects of the geographical environment may also exercise an important influence on the incidence of insurgency, and the role of individual leaders may be decisive as well. So too may be a whole range of cultural influences and the evolution of military tactics and technology. The overall state of great-power relations is relevant also. Obviously much of what has been said in respect of guerrilla war applies to other categories of armed conflict. Thus economic interpretations of warfare are never sufficient in themselves.

On the other hand, many of the additional factors just mentioned seem more likely to determine the location and character of organized violence than they do its global extent. In order to see how far the latter may be governed by economic and social change it may be instructive to refer to an analysis by Robert McNamara, one of the few public figures who has consistently attempted to bridge the gap between development studies and strategic studies alluded to above. In a speech delivered in Montreal in May 1966 he sought to express the correlation now being considered. He said that 32 of the 38 states listed by the World Bank as ' very poor ' (i.e. average annual incomes below $100) had ' suffered significant conflict ' since 1958. So had 69 per cent of the poor nations and 48 per cent of those with middle incomes. But of the 27 nations designated as rich (i.e. at least $750 per capita per annum), only one had experienced major internal upheaval.[31]

---

[31] Council on Foreign Relations, *Documents on American Foreign Relations 1966*, pp. 251–4; see also McNamara's *The Essence of Security* (1968), pp. 145–6.

One does not have to share McNamara's somewhat extreme faith in quantification to be disturbed by his Montreal speech, particularly when it is viewed in the light of some of the more indicative global economic trends. Among the most ominous is the population explosion. Average annual births per 1,000 people are believed to have been higher in most parts of the developing world in the early and middle 1960s than in the previous decade, the increase being especially marked in Southern Asia.[32] UN 'medium projections' predict a growth in the world's population from 2,990 million in 1960 (i.e. 75 per cent more than in 1930) to 4,269 million in 1980 and 5,965 million in 2000, i.e. over five times what it is believed to have been at the time of Malthus![33] By a 'medium projection' the UN means one based on reasonable assumptions about alterations in fertility and mortality. It could, of course, be said that demographic forecasts have sometimes proved even less reliable than those in other branches of macro-economics. In the past, however, UN estimates have not as a rule erred on the side of pessimism.

A particularly disquieting feature of the situation is what has been termed the 'urban implosion'—the supplement to natural urban increase caused by migration from the countryside. Were the 1950–60 rate of urban increase to be maintained, it has been estimated that more than half the world's people would be living in places with 100,000 or more inhabitants by 1990![34] In Latin America, where the degree of urbanization has long been exceptionally high, the percentage of the total population living in towns of 20,000 or more inhabitants had risen from 25 in 1950 to 32 in 1960.[35]

What makes matters worse is the way urban growth tends to focus on capitals and other cities that are already large. Greater Calcutta has some 8 million inhabitants, and a few years ago it was officially estimated that 57 per cent of the multi-member

[32] Lester Pearson & others, *Partners in Development* (London, 1969), Table I, p. 358.

[33] UN, *Provisional Report on World Population Prospects as Assessed in 1963* (ECOSOC, 39th sess., suppl. 9).

[34] Kingsley Davis, 'The Urbanisation of the Human Population', *Scientific American*, Sept. 1965.

[35] UN, *World Population Prospects as Assessed in 1963.*

families had no more than one room to live in.[36] But despite such manifest squalor, it has been said that by the year 2000 the population of Calcutta might be of the order of 50 million.[37]

Even the minimal provision of public services to take account of this urban implosion seems bound to absorb an alarmingly high proportion of the official development budgets of emerging countries. Yet without such provision, some grave security problems might occur. We may, in any event, be about to witness a reversal of the trend away from the urban barricade to the rural ambush that has been perhaps the most prominent element of the evolution of guerrilla warfare since Mao Tse-tung reorganized the Chinese Communist Party in the Kiangsi hills after 1927 in order to transform it into a movement that could 'use the villages to encircle the towns'. As much was suggested by the insurgency against the British in South Arabia, a campaign that was largely concentrated in Aden itself. The Tet offensive of 1968 in Vietnam was a dramatic, albeit unsuccessful, attempt to take the war into the towns in order to inhibit the use of the heavy firepower at the disposal of government and allied forces. Indications of a switch to urban insurgency can also be seen in Latin America.[38]

Sometimes it is argued that the extraordinary gap between birth- and death-rates that has appeared throughout the 'third world' must eventually close because of social evolution and the promotion of family planning. But what is meant by 'eventually'? In most countries in which family-planning programmes have had a discernible effect on the number of births—e.g. Taiwan and Singapore—the birth-rate had already started to fall, apparently in association with a steady improvement in living standards. The evidence from India, in particular, does not suggest that success is as easy to achieve given low incomes, illiteracy, poor communications, and an inadequate medical service. The extraordinary momentum the population explosion has already acquired from the way in which the 'pyramid' of age distribution has developed is another adverse

[36] Nirmal Kumar Bose, 'Calcutta: A Premature Metropolis', *Scientific American*, Sept. 1965.
[37] Davis, *Scientific American*, Sept. 1965.
[38] Che Guevara, *Guerrilla Warfare* (Pelican, 1969), p. 39. See also Carlos Marighella, *Minimanual of the Urban Guerrilla* (Cuba, 1970).

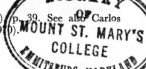

factor. For the combination of widespread maintenance of high birth-rates and an equally widespread diminution in the rates of infant and child mortality has meant that over 40 per cent of the present population is under 15 years old in Africa, Asia, and Latin America, as against a percentage of less than 30 in Europe and North America. By 1980 the number of women in their 20s (i.e. their most fertile decade) in these continents is authoritatively expected to be double what it was in 1965.[39]

It is moreover essential that national incomes in the 'third world' should do substantially more than merely keep abreast of population growth. For the probability is that what Adlai Stevenson called the 'revolution of rising expectations' will not only continue but will accelerate. Formal education is still far from universal, even at primary school level; and while a continuation of this state of affairs would clearly be intolerable, a further broadening of the educational base will necessarily bring more young people into at least vicarious contact with more affluent ways of life. Likewise the ubiquitous urban inflow, though itself largely an expression of the quest for a more free and colourful life, may generate more aspirations than it satisfies.

Then again, such conspicuous and exotic examples of Western consumption as supersonic airliners and space programmes may well provoke intense envy within any community not making tangible progress towards the elimination of primary poverty, just as the impact of Western affluence in a broader sense will be enhanced by more contact with it. Thus the dramatic increase in the number of wireless receivers in use that took place throughout Africa and Asia and Latin America in the 1950s may soon be followed by a comparable one in respect of television sets. What makes this prognosis more plausible and significant is the swift progress now under way in the application to global communications of orbiting satellites. Because of their own wavelength characteristics, television signals depend on these satellites for long-distance transmission, e.g. across the Atlantic or Pacific.

As expectations rise, they embrace an ever-greater variety of goods and services; they are also much concerned with social and political emancipation. Every country in the world has to

[39] Population Reference Bureau, Washington, Apr. 1969.

grapple with the challenge thereby presented. At the same time, however, most of them are in the throes of a still more urgent struggle—that to furnish a more adequate food supply. When due allowance is made not only for a possible population increase of 75–80 per cent but also for a need to eliminate malnutrition and, in addition, to provide for a significant general increase in spending power per head, the rise in demand for food in the developing countries expected between 1962 and 1985 in the FAO's Indicative World Plan of 1969 is no less than 142 per cent, i.e. 3·9 per cent per annum.[40] Not to meet it might be to pave the way for extensive violence, much of which inevitably would flow across international borders.

Only a short time ago some well-informed observers believed that a Malthusian catastrophe along these lines was already virtually unavoidable.[41] In 1965 and 1966 harvests were so poor that per capita food output in Africa, the Far East, and Latin America was little if any higher than the average for the late 1930s. Then in 1967 food production in the developing countries rose no less than 6 per cent. This rather remarkable recovery was largely thanks to high prices and good weather and to the maintenance of a general improvement in methods. But in addition several-fold increases in output per acre were locally registered in various countries (including India and Pakistan) by the use, in conjunction with irrigation and lavish applications of fertilizer, of new varieties of maize, rice, and wheat. Since 1967, moreover, the spread of this new husbandry has sharply accelerated.

Admittedly the quality of the new rice is substandard in several respects, the strains so far developed being rather prone to disease and yielding a kernel that is regarded as inferior in taste and consistency. True also an improvement in grain yield is unlikely in this decade to have a decisive effect on the chief shortage because this is usually a protein rather than a carbohydrate deficiency. Though certain new wheats will be substantially richer in protein than are existing types, they will not be available for some years. And the most serious shortfall

[40] *New Scientist*, 23 Oct. 1969.
[41] W. & P. Paddock, *Famine—1975!* (London, 1968). See also Professor René Dumont's address to the Africa Centre (*Observer*, 10 Dec. 1967).

is expected in protein of animal origin, an important ingredient of any well-balanced diet.

Nevertheless, when to this incipient ' green revolution ' is added the scope that exists—at any rate in principle—for increasing acreages, controlling pests, and exploiting other innovations, an attractive picture might be formed of bountiful years ahead, an impression which might be strengthened by the expectation that by the middle 1970s the advanced Western nations will normally have larger grain surpluses than today. But a merely cursory examination of the situation is enough to reveal that, in reality, a decisive breakthrough is neither imminent nor certain. Political and financial factors seem to make the prospect of a large-scale flow of food from the West doubtful. Between 1955 and 1965 agricultural output in the third world increased by a modest 2·8 per cent per annum, i.e. at a rate well below likely requirements for the next ten to fifteen years. [42] A shortage of specialists and of working capital often slows down the application of new techniques, as does the bias against the countryside still so prevalent among governmental élites. Another constraint is the failure in many cases to implement land reform. And although religious and social taboos are being eroded the whole time, there are still many areas in which they militate against economic realism over such questions as the rearing of pigs and cattle.

Nor should it be assumed that agricultural progress is necessarily a harbinger of political stability. Since the improved grain husbandry referred to above can only really flourish in areas that are well-watered and also possessed of a tolerably sophisticated economic and social structure, it might conceivably accentuate regional disparities, for example within India or other large and heterogeneous territories. It could also operate, in conjunction with the general spread of mechanized farming, to elevate further the ' kulaks ' or ' improving landlord ' groups and to accelerate the flow of landless labourers from the countryside to the cities. [43] Any of these effects would tend to arouse

[42] *New Scientist*, 23 Oct. 1969.

[43] Perhaps the projections for the urban implosion referred to above should be regarded as conservative in that they were made before the new grain began to make an impact!

acute political hostility. It is possible that some of the roots of the current unrest in West Bengal may lie in the way in which, partly thanks to the failure of successive Congress governments fully to implement their promises of land reform, the incipient ' green revolution ' has widened economic differentials in the countryside.

Thus already this wave of innovation may serve to remind us that there is no simple causal link between economic development and ' political stability ', i.e. evolutionary as opposed to revolutionary political change. What does seem clear is that economic growth will not be the basis for the orderly progress of any society unless it be sufficiently rapid and broadly based materially to benefit a wide cross-section of that society. To favour the best-placed landowners does not contribute to stability. Nor is it helpful to free men from the drudgery of manual farm labour only to provide them with no alternative livelihood. A man without work in a congested city may pose a bigger political problem than one without food in a village.

It is, however, difficult to believe that fast yet well-balanced growth can be achieved without large-scale assistance on the part of the advanced industrial nations. The big question is whether this will be forthcoming in sufficient quantity. The provision of direct economic aid has been cramped in recent years by a mood of introversion in some of the leading Western countries and by their own financial anxieties. Measured as a percentage of the combined GNPs of donor states, the net annual flow of government and private capital from the OECD area (which, for this purpose, includes Australia and Japan) was only 0·79 in 1968 and 0·72 in 1969[44] as against 0·96 in 1961.[45] In monetary terms there was about a 45 per cent increase, but this compared with a rise of well over 60 per cent in the recorded value of international trade. What makes this lag even more serious than might otherwise be the case is the continuing geographical imbalance in aid distribution; between 1964 and 1967 Chile received US$14·5 per capita in official bilateral and multilateral aid, whereas India received only $2·5.[46] It is, however,

[44] OECD, Press Release, 28 July 1970.
[45] OECD, *1969 Review: Development Assistance* (1969), p. 206.
[46] Pearson, *Partners in Development*, Table 27, p. 392.

probable that the Indian economy is already sufficiently mature to enable India, even at quite short notice, to put to good use two or three times the aid now being supplied, and during the next few years a number of other poor countries are also likely to improve their ability usefully to absorb capital inflows.[47] Not to give them the chance to do this might be to leave them with a dangerous surplus of human energy. Anxiety on this score is not assuaged by warnings that the number of totally unemployed workers in Asia, Africa, and Latin America could easily rise from 75 million to 300 million in the course of this decade.[48]

One conclusion that emerges from this study of the interaction between the arms race and the problem of development is that there is an urgent need to bring to a more appropriate focus the now highly fashionable activity of predicting the future of human society. For a good deal of this prognostic effort, at least as far as the more synoptic assessments are concerned, is concentrated on the year 2000 or some time thereafter, a predilection that is to be regretted on two main counts. One is that it is unrealistic to expect forecasts more than ten or fifteen years ahead ever to make a worthwhile impact on those who shape government policies. Another is the tendency for too long-range a projection to induce euphoric complacency on technological grounds. It is all too easy to demonstrate that, if mankind does get as far as the twenty-first century, science and technology should be in a position to provide its members with enviable measures of affluence and leisure. What is less certain is whether, in fact, civilization will reach AD 2000 in a recognizable form. Thus it is to 1985 that we should direct most attention.

[47] A. H. Hanson in George Cunningham, ed., *Britain and the World in the Seventies: a Collection of Fabian Essays* (1970).

[48] *The Times*, 13 Oct. 1970.

Suggestions for Further Reading

Beaton, Leonard. *Must the bomb spread?* Penguin, 1966.

Bridger, Gordon and Maurice de Soissons. *Famine in retreat?* London, Dent, 1970.

Brown, Lester R. *Seeds of change: the green revolution and development in the 1970s.* New York, Praeger, 1970.

Calder, Nigel. *The environment game.* London, Secker, 1967.

Campbell, Arthur. *Guerrillas: a history and analysis.* London, Barker, 1967.

Chayes, Abram and Jerome B. Weisner, eds. *ABM: an evaluation of the decision to deploy an anti-ballistic missile system.* New York, Harper, 1969.

Cunningham, George, ed. *Britain and the world in the seventies: a collection of Fabian essays.* London, Weidenfeld & Nicolson, 1970.

Garthoff, Raymond. *Soviet military policy.* London, Faber, 1966.
ISS. *The military balance,* 1970–1. London, 1970.

Kahn, Herman and A. J. Wiener. *The year 2000.* London, Collier-Macmillan, 1968.

Lapp, Ralph. *Arms beyond doubt; the tyranny of weapons technology.* New York, Cowles Book Co., 1970.

McNamara, Robert S. *The essence of security.* London, Hodder, 1968.

Sokolovskii, V. D., ed. *Military strategy; Soviet doctrine and concepts.* London, 1963.

Stockholm International Peace Research Inst. *SIPRI yearbook of world armaments and disarmament.* London, Duckworth, 1970.

3

THE SECURITY FUNCTIONS OF THE UNITED NATIONS

Alan James

THE first purpose of the UN, as stated in Article 1 of its Charter, is ' To maintain international peace and security '. Its makers therefore emphasized the pacific settlement of disputes, and also the regulation of armaments—recalling two parts of the popular inter-war triptych, arbitration, security, and disarmament. The events leading to the Second World War, however, resulted in the third part—security—being singled out as deserving of particular attention. Hence the core of the 1945 plan is its provision for ' effective collective measures ' to deal with threats to the peace, breaches of the peace, and acts of aggression. Pre-eminently, the UN was envisaged as a security organization, indeed, as *the* security organization of the postwar world.

Primary responsibility for its central task was laid on the appropriately-named Security Council, made up of five permanent members (Britain, China, France, the Soviet Union, and the United States) and six (later ten) other states elected for a two-year term. It was empowered to deploy air, sea, and land forces to maintain or restore peace, and all members of the UN agreed to accept and carry out its decisions. Clearly, the new Organization was not intended to be short of teeth. But before this imposing arrangement can be brought into operation, two conditions have to be satisfied. The first is the conclusion, under Article 43 of the Charter, of special agreements between UN members and the Security Council regarding the forces and facilities they will make available on its call. Failing such agreements the Council cannot require members to put armed force at its disposal when a crisis occurs (and the UN has no military resources of its own). But even if it has the right to demand assistance the Council must, secondly, decide to do so, which means that none of the permanent members must be opposed to that course. For on matters of this kind each of them is constitutionally able to prevent a Council decision being taken, or, to use the more familiar expression, to exercise its veto.

These conditions, however, are less important than they might seem. It is hardly to be expected that the absence of special agreements—and as yet none have been concluded—will stand in the way of UN action in circumstances where it is otherwise possible, i.e. where some members are anxious to fight in the Organization's name and where no permanent Council member is prepared to vote against their doing so. The lack of a special agreement may provide a useful excuse for a state which is reluctant to join in collective action, but it is no obstacle to a willing participant. This was shown, albeit somewhat unusually, in 1950 when the Soviet boycott (over the issue of Chinese representation) enabled the Security Council to take action which resulted in a UN force assisting South Korea against Northern aggression. As no special agreements had been made the Council had no right to call a force into being; all it could do was to recommend that UN members help South Korea. But as the necessary political will was present, the organization of a UN fighting force gave rise to no problems.

The veto would appear to offer greater obstructive possibilities, inasmuch as it can prevent the Council launching an operation which is favoured by a majority of its members. But putting the matter in this way can obscure the point that the UN was based on the premiss of the continued unity of the victorious Great powers. It was not intended that the Organization's military potential should be used by one such power against another, or even against the other's friends. Hence the veto was deliberately included as a means of obstruction, as a way of signifying that the Great could not agree—and therefore that action, if any, would have to be taken outside the UN.

It might have been that an occasional stultifying disagreement would not have prevented the UN from acting as an effective security organization in most crises. But the onset of the cold war, and the deep mutual distrust which it reflected, made it very clear at an early date that the Organization would be quite unable to operate as planned. The fortuitous circumstances which resulted in the UN playing a military role in Korea led some to hope that it need not be written off as a purveyor of security, and their thoughts turned to the possibility of using the General Assembly for this purpose. Here all members are represented; decisions on important matters are taken by a two-thirds majority; and Western states and sympathizers made up the overwhelming bulk of its membership. Accordingly, in November 1950, against strong Communist opposition, the Assembly passed an American-sponsored draft (the Uniting for Peace Resolution) by which it asserted the right to make recommendations regarding the use of armed force when the Security Council was blocked by a veto.

But very little came of this attempt at the *de facto* amendment of the Charter. However compliant the Assembly might be, there was little doubt that the security of the West could be organized with more efficiency in an exclusive body, or a series of such bodies. Thus Korea remained the exception proving the rule that the UN could not provide security when each of its two chief members regarded the other as the major threat to international peace. Equally, the division of the world into two heavily armed camps prevented any progress towards the regulation of armaments. It was still possible for the UN to urge the pacific settlement of disputes and sometimes to offer its services towards this end. But the East-West conflict meant that except, perhaps, on peripheral issues, there was little hope of the UN acting as an authoritative peace-maker. Thus within a few years of its foundation, there seemed no prospect of the UN fulfilling its important security functions.

The 1950s brought no change in this respect. The UN had a new lease of life from about the middle of the decade, with a sudden increase in membership and an emphasis on what was called ' peace-keeping ' activity. Additionally, Soviet policy showed a marked flexibility following the death of Stalin in 1953. But the basic hostility between East and West remained, with the consequence that the UN was unable to embark upon the role for which it had been cast in 1945. Nor did the following decade alter this situation. But the 1960s did see the growth of something in the nature of a *détente* between the two super-powers, the beginning of which seemed to be precipitated by their eye-ball confrontation in October 1962 over the installation of Soviet missiles in Cuba. The development by both sides of an invulnerable second-strike nuclear capacity assisted the process, as, no doubt, did the growing differences between the Soviet Union and China. However, while the overall position was widely thought to justify the proclamation of the end of the cold war, there was little evidence of close co-operative activity, of the kind of fruit a *détente* might be expected to bear. This was commonly attributed to the American involvement in Vietnam. Hence the new Nixon policy of cautious disengagement has given rise to hope that the super-power *détente* will flourish in the 1970s, and, more particularly, that one sign of this will be the breathing of much-delayed life into the Charter's security scheme.

However, this assumes not only that the new decade will see a good deal of joint super-power action, but also that that action will often be channelled through or conducted under the auspices of the UN. Even if the first assumption proves correct, the second by no means follows. For just as the major contestants in the cold war preferred to conduct their conflict without the benefit of the UN's advice, so the powers acting in concert could choose to operate outside the world organization. The Locarno tea-parties of the middle and late 1920s—those private gatherings of the Great at Geneva, which were alleged to take much important business away from the League Council—were to a considerable extent indicative of this response, and it is improbable that the passage of time has greatly reduced the appeal of such an approach. Discussion in a small, exclusive group beyond the public eye and ear generally seems so very suitable to those whose rank is sufficiently elevated to assure their participation.

Moreover, there are some issues which lend themselves particularly well to this treatment. A case in point is the current discussion between the Soviet Union and the United States regarding the limitation of strategic arms. Likewise, the long negotiations which culminated in the 1963 treaty banning many nuclear tests were essentially between the same two powers plus Britain, and the two super-powers were the crucial parties in the talks which led up to the 1968 Nuclear Non-Proliferation

Treaty. However, from 1962 onwards the test-ban talks were associated with the Eighteen-Nation Disarmament Conference at Geneva, a body which has close links with the UN though it is not formally part of it, and from time to time the prospective parties were urged on by the General Assembly. In respect of the non-proliferation negotiations the Eighteen-Nation Conference and the Assembly played a somewhat more important role, which was perhaps to be expected in view of the subject-matter. But it is also an indication of the extent to which the UN is now established on the international scene. Thus it is accepted on all sides that the Organization as a whole may have a legitimate claim to be heard, and sometimes consulted, on matters which are the major responsibility of the great powers. The move towards a *détente* during the 1960s has not obviously hindered this development, so there is no reason to postulate an invariably inverse relationship between the two. Accordingly, if Soviet-American relations continue to improve, it remains very possible that both states will continue to look to the UN for the endorsement of their joint and several policies, and that they will occasionally take advantage of the opportunity of acting co-operatively, in one way or another, under the aegis of this socially approved and ambitious Organization.

It has, for example, been suggested in several quarters that an improving international climate might result in the Security Council taking the kind of strong action against aggression which was originally assigned to it. There is little that it can do about threats to the peace emanating from the super-powers—an area which was in any event never intended to lie within its competence. But as the Soviet Union and the United States develop a mutual interest in general stability, so there opens up the possibility that they might use the Council to further this end, maintaining or restoring peace through UN fighting forces which could well include a significant great-power element. In this connexion proposals have been made for renewed consideration to be given to the negotiation of special agreements under Article 43 of the Charter and for the reactivation of the Military Staff Committee, which was meant to advise and assist the Council on this and related matters.

The implementation of these ideas, however, presupposes

that the major powers will see international disturbances in a serious and virtually identical light, and also, probably, that at least one of them will be prepared to go to considerable trouble in the cause of order. Experience to date is not encouraging with regard to either of these factors, and as yet there is no instance of their conjunction. In 1931 Japan's invasion of Manchuria may have been thought regrettable, but it was hardly regarded as a grave threat to their interests by the leading members of the League. Peace, evidently, was divisible, especially when its breach occurred far from the area on which the League's attention was focused. Italy's attack on Ethiopia in 1935 was nearer home, in several senses, and it is to the credit of the overwhelming majority of League members that they were prepared to condemn the aggressor and go some way towards the execution of their consequential obligation to impose economic sanctions. But there was no rush towards sacrificial action, nor any sign that the presumptive leaders— Britain and France—suffered much frustration on account of the lack of enthusiasm of their fellows. Enthusiasm, in fact, was pre-eminently what was lacking once the issues were lowered from the emotional to the practical level. Sympathy was not enough to align the League with Ethiopia, especially when Italy's power and diplomatic position led a number of important members to conclude that it was in their interest to inconvenience the aggressor as little as possible.

It was not, in fact, until 1950 that a quasi-universal organization resorted to really tough measures against a misbehaving state, when a UN force was established to resist North Korea's attack on the southern part of this divided country. The vast bulk of the force (excepting its South Korean element) was American, reflecting the determination of the United States not to let the rival camp chalk up a victory—not even in Korea, from which she had earlier appeared to disinterest herself. But the Soviet Union was on the other diplomatic side and, as has been noted, it was only the fortuitous absence of her delegate which enabled the Security Council to throw the UN's blue mantle over the anti-red initiative which had already been taken by the United States. The pro-Western character of the resultant operation has led some analysts to say that it was not a proper example of collective security. As against this view it can be argued that legitimate institutional action is not necessarily confined to that which is approved by all members, and that drastic security operations by a body like the UN are almost bound to serve the interests of some states to a disproportionate degree, such states naturally showing most enthusiasm for the theoretically common cause. At the practical level, however, it is certainly the case that collective security is very difficult when the major powers are deeply divided, and particularly so for the UN on account of its constitutional structure. And although the super-states have not always been at odds since Korea, and, indeed, have moved much closer in recent years, there has been no case where their common mind has been supplemented by a willingness to take or endorse forceful action.

In itself, neither this, nor the earlier experience of the UN and of the League before it, is a sufficient basis for the assumption that the powers are unlikely to use the UN as a significant security organization. Caution is also enjoined by the fact that international politics can develop very speedily, and in unexpected ways. There are, however, two other factors which clearly suggest that the balance of probability is at present against the revival of the UN's security scheme.

The first of these relates to the nature of the super-power *détente*. There is no doubt that the powers have a strong mutual interest in the maintenance of peace among themselves, that they are discovering a shared concern with regard to the limiting of competition in strategic arms, and that they have demonstrated a common desire to curtail the spread of nuclear weapons. It can also be said, correctly, that they have a general interest in international stability, but beyond this point the *détente* sometimes becomes rather hard to discern. Both powers may be agreed on the need for peace in the Middle East, but evidently they are far from agreed as to the desirable outline of that peace, or even as to the first interim measure which might be taken towards it. Thus they are in no position to act jointly *vis-à-vis* the local participants. Likewise with regard to the Indian sub-continent. Here the three-weeks war between India and Pakistan in 1965 enabled them to show their common concern about the restoration of peace, but they had nothing substantive to offer, or to insist upon, so far as a settlement of the basic problem of Kashmir was concerned.

Moreover, such negative agreement as has been possible in these two areas should not obscure the fact that for many purposes the Soviet Union and the United States still see themselves very much as competitors, and not in any too friendly a sense either. Each is still seeking the support and sympathy of the non-aligned states, as can be seen from their speeches at the UN and elsewhere. Each is prepared to capitalize on the embarrassments of the other, as was seen in respect of American intervention in the Dominican Republic in 1965 and of Soviet intervention in Czechoslovakia in 1968. The reasons for this may have partly been to do with domestic politics and the demands and expectations of allies, but none the less it is an important qualification on the alleged growing warmth of the East-West relationship. Each still feels, or feels obliged to purport to feel, ideologically distinct—and the Soviet Union, particularly, has shown considerable embarrassment in the last year or two at suggestions that there has been such a convergence between the great powers that now there is not much to choose between them. Each continues to be deeply suspicious of the other, so much so that even the most cautious move towards improving the UN's peace-keeping procedures is stymied by the Soviet Union in order to prevent the possibility that the United States might use her superior position in the Organization to employ military observers or non-fighting forces to Soviet disadvantage. In short, the *détente* may be developing some depth, but its effective lateral range remains very limited. Its sudden extension is not to be excluded, especially in consequence of Sino-Soviet developments (although that would also depend on American co-operation, which may not be totally or easily forthcoming). But East-West relations at the opening of the 1970s do not appear to herald a wide-ranging concert of the powers. The Soviet Union and the United States may sometimes be able to agree on a call for peace, but they show little sign of that degree of trust and co-operation which is required if they are to put a great-power fighting force into the field, or to establish and control one made up of contingents from lesser states. For this reason alone, therefore, there does not seem much chance that the intentions of the Charter with regard to security will be fulfilled.

Quite apart from this consideration, however, there is a second factor which points towards the same conclusion. It is that the kind of conflict with which, pre-eminently, the UN, like the League before it, was meant to deal is nowadays relatively rare. Both institutions were established to cope with overt attempts at direct aggrandizement by regular military means, or, to put it more shortly, wars of conquest. It was, for example, the First World War which the Covenant makers had in mind as the sort of problem which would in future benefit from organized counter-action. Likewise, it was the further German attempt at territorial expansion which in 1945 was regarded as typical of the issues which would need to be attended to by the guardians of the new order. But in the event this traditional type of threat to international peace has gone out of fashion.

A plethora of exceedingly destructive weapons may have contributed significantly to this result in respect of the super-powers' relations with each other, while among some lesser states a shortage of offensive weapons of any sort may have had a similar effect. Additionally, the many new states of Africa must have been influenced by the consideration that, as in the case of Latin America long since, an emphasis on the legitimacy of original boundaries would be to everyone's benefit by helping to avoid conflicts which otherwise would probably be as costly and weakening as they would be numerous. However, the disrepute into which war as an instrument of national policy has fallen can also be attributed to developments in the realm of ideas, in that this old-established procedure is now widely regarded as improper. This is partly due, without doubt, to practical matters of the kind already mentioned. But the presently popular idea is not a new one, having found early representation in religious and moral thought, and recently it has received vast secular nourishment from the concept of self-determination. For the now-orthodox view that all nations have the right to govern themselves means that territory can no longer be regarded as in the nature of a marketable commodity, to be bought—i.e. annexed—by those with the requisite resources. Moreover, this restriction on the freedom of states to act up to the limit of their strength is further curtailed by the dogma that in the post-colonial period nations are defined by state boundaries.

Thus large-scale territorial acquisition can only be made by those who, in addition to the normal costs of such an enterprise, are prepared to run the gauntlet of hostile opinion, which these days is not treated as a negligible factor. Account has also to be taken of the fact that 'normal costs' have been stepped up of late because of the ideological hostility to conquest. For the view that people should be governed by their own representatives (however spurious the representative character of the governors) may be expected to increase the resentment of those who find themselves subject to a foreign sovereign, and to provide a convenient ground for opposition to the occupying regime, thus increasing the difficulty of its task. Hence it is not surprising that straightforward aggressive war is no longer regarded as an attractive option even where the balance of forces is very favourable, and that when armed force is used or makes its presence felt it is commonly accompanied by numerous qualifications and is not followed by the formal changes which once would have been customary. Thus the Soviet Union did not establish an empire in East Europe after 1945. She was supposedly invited into Hungary in 1956 and into Czechoslovakia in 1968, and in the latter case used the Warsaw Pact to collectivize the invasion. Likewise in the Western hemisphere America's intervention in the Dominican Republic in 1965 was followed by a hastily erected Organization of American States umbrella, with formal deference being paid to the sovereignty of the 'host' state throughout. The same state allowed Japan to retain 'residual sovereignty' in Okinawa after the Second World War, and in 1956 her leading allies professed, among other things, to be serving the international interest in their attempt to 'safeguard' the Suez Canal. Apart from the old city of Jerusalem, which has tremendous emotional significance for Jewry, Israel has not formally annexed any of her 1967 acquisitions at the expense of the Arabs, and even with regard to Jerusalem she acted in an underhand and somewhat embarrassed way. The state which is generally regarded as least mindful of world opinion and international conventions—Communist China—withdrew from India after her speedy incursion in 1962.

Even, therefore, if the *détente* was such as to permit the exercise of force by the powers in support of peace, it is unlikely that the UN would often be given the opportunity of acting in circumstances which would be familiar to the Organization's founders. This does not exclude the possibility of the Charter being used as a basis for action in respect of other sorts of conflict, but it happens that those which are now common are not ones which are likely, in the present political climate, to attract the collective application of security measures. Disputes regarding self-determination, and the allied issue of racialism, for example, do not appear on the UN's agenda in the context of how to assist a beleaguered state. Rather the UN is anxious to alter the situation in a way which the chief states involved—Portugal and South Africa—regard as seriously detrimental to their security, and South Africa's claim to this effect can hardly be denied. For this is a class of case in which the UN is much more concerned with the majority's interpretation of justice or freedom than with territorial integrity. This was interestingly demonstrated in December 1969 when the General Assembly decided to issue two sets of stamps to mark the Organization's 25th anniversary, one bearing an originally proposed theme, ' Peace and Progress ', and the other with the theme which was now preferred: ' Peace, Justice and Progress '.

Another type of dispute in which it is very unlikely that the UN will make any substantive move is one which concerns a country's political complexion and therefore, supposedly, its international attitude. Correlations of this kind have been one of the hallmarks of the ideologically inclined international society of the mid-twentieth century, with the result that internal upsets, or their prospect, have sometimes elicited a highly controversial response from interested outsiders. By virtue of this very fact there has been little chance of firm and effective UN action—either an insistence on non-intervention or decisive intervention on one side. The difficulties in the way of any such course were vividly exemplified in the Congo crisis of 1960 when the UN, already involved in the country, endeavoured to assist the cause of law and order by acting in a way which was to the grave detriment of the left-wing prime minister and greatly favoured the moderate president. The outcome was that the Soviet Union immediately called for Dag Hammarskjöld's head and proposed a radical refashioning of the office of Secretary-General. A similar lesson is offered by the unsuccessful efforts of the powers to prevent intervention in the Spanish civil war in the late 1930s. The opening of the 1970s finds the international climate appreciably more relaxed than a decade earlier and also than in the years immediately preceding the Second World War. But it may be doubted whether, even under a continually improving *détente*, the powers would be able to hold the line on a question of intervention. It would be a very unusual situation in which none of them saw a worthwhile profit accruing from partial activity in an internal struggle which promised to have important external repercussions. Even the Vienna powers of 1815 were not as united as that.

The remaining issues which in recent years have involved the threat or use of force, and which therefore, on the face of it, would seem to be suitable for the UN's authoritative intervention, are border claims and incidents. And, as always, such disputes have by no means been uncommon, forming an appreciable proportion of the total number. But conflicts of this sort generally remain limited, in terms of both purpose and physical activity, and so do not precipitate questions regarding the mobilization of an international force to repel aggression. The post-1945 period has been orthodox in this respect, thus providing further support for the argument that the kind of tension with which the UN's scheme for collective security was chiefly erected to deal has so far been most noticeable by its absence.

However, what contemporary frontier, and other, disputes may be thought to stand in need of, and what the UN may be able to provide, is an insistence that they be not prosecuted by force of arms, or that any armed conflict to which they have given rise should be brought to an immediate halt. This does not amount to the settlement of the issue, and may not even prove to be a step in that direction. But nevertheless there is a widespread disposition nowadays to deprecate fighting, especially other people's fights, and the UN has been found to be a convenient and appropriate medium through which this feeling can be expressed. Of course, even a united call for a cease-fire from the Assembly or Council may be ignored by belligerents. In that event there is little the UN can do about it short of physical involvement, which is not easy to arrange even against clear-cut aggression and would be much harder if what was required was the separation of combatants—a much less pressing but perhaps a not much less costly task. If, however, the parties are not totally committed to the continuation of their war, a UN demand that they call a halt may help to tip the decision-making scales in that direction, particularly if the world organization can muster an impressive amount of political weight behind its decree. Should the UN be acting through the Security Council that requirement would almost certainly be satisfied, for although it is now theoretically possible for the Council to take a decision without any of the permanent members voting for it, such an event is politically unlikely.

There are instances of the UN acting in just this way with the desired result. It does not follow that the outcome was due to the UN's action, but it can at least be said that the institutional factor should not be dismissed out of hand. In July 1948, for example, the Council ordered the parties to the war of Palestinian succession to cease fire within three days. Here the Soviet Union abstained, but Britain, France, and the United States were all strongly behind the resolution. In September 1965 all the powers concurred in demanding that India and Pakistan cease fire, and the resolution went on to specify the day and time at which it was to come into force. Two years later, in the Six-Day War, the Council was unanimous in addressing the contestants in similar terms. The last two cases are particularly interesting in this context as they illustrate a prominent feature of the UN's history during the 1960s: a return to the Security Council, in the sense that the powers are now sometimes using that body as a vehicle for their co-operation, in marked contrast to its earlier employment as a mere recorder of their dissension. If the *détente* continues, it is to be expected that they will from time to time find that they have a joint interest in stability and that they will occasionally be

glad to resort to the Council as a means of expressing, channel-
ling, and legitimizing their common will. They may still do so
even in the event of the Peking regime succeeding to China's
permanent seat on the Security Council, for it is not to be
assumed that Communist China will necessarily be opposed
to order in all circumstances. And where a veto prevents the
Council from proceeding in this way, the other powers might
well agree to resort to the Assembly, in the manner of the
Western majority in the 1950s.

On the other hand it may be found, as it has been in the
past, that in this kind of situation it is not enough for the UN
just to utter its will. Additionally some action on the ground
may be required. Thus in 1948 the Palestinian cease-fire—or
truce as it was called—was supervised by a body of UN observers,
who remained to watch over the armistices which were signed
in the following year by Israel and each of the surrounding
Arab states. It was hoped that by helping to maintain calm
they would prepare the way for a settlement. This hope was
not entirely fulfilled, but at least the observers were able, then,
and for almost twenty years thereafter, to secure as peaceful
a front as was permitted by the political contest. Accidental
war escalating out of a local clash was something which they
were able to prevent. Both facets of the UN's potential in this
respect were displayed following the Indo-Pakistani war of
1965. An international group of military observers proceeded
to the Indian sub-continent as soon as the war was over, did
what they could to maintain the cease-fire for some months, and
then assisted in the restoration of the *status quo ante* by facilitating
the smooth withdrawal of troops. By contrast, the UN military
observers who were established on the post-Six-Day-War cease-
fire line between Israel and the UAR have neither contributed to a
settlement nor been able to maintain quiet along the line, for
the governments involved have latterly been behaving in a very
belligerent manner.

Since the UN's part in the Suez crisis of 1956 action of this
sort has gone by the name of peace-keeping. It has been based
on the principle of consent, in that there has been no question
of the UN forcing its way into a country or of its operating in a
manner which has not been permitted by the host. Equally,

whatever the host's desires, the UN's job has not included fighting against its enemies—not, at least, against its international enemies. With the partial exception of the Congo, the Organization's task has been to operate within the context of such local agreement as can be found, helping the parties to move towards or execute a settlement, or to implement their desire if not for peace at least for the avoidance of war. And it has been a notable characteristic of peace-keeping during this period that, except for the unusual case of the UN Force in Cyprus, which includes a British contingent, and a small continuing American and French representation in the Palestinian truce observation team, the UN has not drawn on any of the Security Council's permanent members for personnel. But the major powers, especially the Western ones and the United States pre-eminently, have had other roles of great importance, some of them always having been to the fore in the authorization process and with financial support and logistical backing. Accordingly, it might well be thought that UN peace-keeping should be among the beneficiaries of a strengthening great-power *détente*, being a process which depends to a large extent on the powers and which can be used by them to serve their, arguably benign, purposes.

But as against this, note has to be taken of the fact that currently there is a good deal of disenchantment and pessimism over UN peace-keeping, casting a doubt on the likelihood of its utilization however close the great powers get. In part this flows from the UN's present impotence in the Middle East, where its Mediator can make no progress and its truce supervisors along the Suez Canal are reduced to keeping the growing score of gross and calculated infringements of the cease-fire. Then, too, the circumstances surrounding the withdrawal of the UN Emergency Force from the UAR border with Israel in May 1967 did nothing, in some eyes, to redeem the Organization's standing, such critics arguing that the Secretary-General ought at least to have prevaricated and might have tried to take a stand in face of President Nasser's peremptory demand for the winding-up of the Force. This points to a more general line of criticism: that the present Secretary-General is altogether too cautious and self-effacing for the UN to be able to play a very positive role. He is contrasted unfavourably with his predecessor, whose subtlety and thrust is represented as having had much to do with the supposed heyday of peace-keeping in the latter part of the 1950s.

It is true that Hammarskjöld deserves very great credit for the dynamism and ingenuity which he displayed during the Suez crisis, which bore fruit in the patching-up (and subsequently prophylactic) Emergency Force. He was also responsible for the speedy expansion of the Observer Group in the Lebanon in the late summer of 1958, and had a large hand in the UN's rapid and substantial response to the appeal from the Congo in 1960. But it is also worth noticing that the build-up of the Observer Group served little apparent purpose, and that in the case of the Congo the UN soon found it had bitten off more than it could comfortably digest. One result was that the Secretary-General, identifying himself with a course of action which was bitterly opposed by the Soviet Union, lost much of his usefulness as the Organization's chief official. At the time of his tragic death his star was probably in irreversible decline. U Thant, on the other hand, is still acceptable to all the powers after nine years in office. This is not necessarily a commendation, nor is it entirely due to his own achievements. But he can hardly be charged with having presided over a decaying UN or of having been inactive himself in the peace-keeping field. Since his arrival the Organization has disengaged itself from the Congo, after taking action which Britain and France would have been unlikely to stomach a year or two earlier. It has administered West New Guinea for seven months and so assisted in the ending of the long-standing quarrel over its ownership. It has dispatched observer missions to the Yemen and the Indian subcontinent, and a force to Cyprus. It has re-established its presence on two of the four Middle Eastern cease-fire lines after the Six-Day War. And in all these developments the Secretary-General played a part, sometimes a very substantial one. In reply it can be said that U Thant permitted the UN to suffer a severe setback by his action in the crisis of May 1967. But it is not at all likely that the outcome of President Nasser's demand for the withdrawal of UNEF would have been any different whatever the Secretary-General, or the UN's political organs, had done.

The fact is that the UN is there to be utilized and discarded as disputants see fit. During the last few years it happens to have been discarded in one or two areas, and over the same period it has not embarked on any large new operations. But this does not mean that in future crises the parties will write off the UN as a possible source of help. U Thant's record since 1961 should be sufficient to controvert any idea that the Secretary-General is uninterested in peace-keeping. Nor, it should be obvious, is there any warrant for the view that the Organization is, as it were, out of practice and therefore incapable of effective action. It is, after all, continuing operations of some importance in Kashmir and Cyprus. If the UN mystique had suffered a serious reverse, there might be some ground for pessimism. But that has not happened, at least not to a significant degree. From which it may be concluded that in suitable instances the parties will continue to look to the UN for impartial assistance of the kind which has been afforded in the past.

Whether the UN responds positively to requests for peace-keeping operations, however, depends to a considerable extent on the attitude of the major powers, and in this connexion there are two further grounds for arguing that the outlook is bleak. The first draws attention to the fact that the permanent members of the Security Council are by no means agreed on certain important issues relating to this aspect of the UN's activities. It was, after all, the refusal of two of them—France and the Soviet Union—to pay their share of peace-keeping costs which resulted in the ' lame-duck ' session of the Assembly in 1964–5. The immediate crisis was resolved (at the expense of the Charter) but the French and Soviet reservations about peace-keeping remained. In consequence, the Committee which was appointed to produce guidelines for future operations has so far failed to reach any substantive agreement even with regard to military observers, let alone UN forces. Nor has the Secretariat felt able to engage in contingency planning with a view to improving the Organization's peace-keeping performance. One symptom of this is the vacancy which has existed since the end of 1968 in the post of Military Adviser to the Secretary-General. The failure to fill it can be explained on the ground that the UN's current requirements in this area are insufficient to justify the employment of a high-ranking officer. But it is also indicative of the way in which political factors place a taboo on any consideration, by the Secretariat, of the UN's future requirements and how they might be met. Even, therefore, if the Secretary-General had no such role in mind for a new Adviser, his mere appointment would, in the present situation, arouse suspicion in influential quarters, with the very probable result that for a while the Secretariat would find life full of new difficulties.

This might suggest that UN peace-keeping does not have much of a future, despite the prospects of *détente*. There is also a second, more general argument which points in the same direction. And it does so not despite but because of the recent improvement in great-power relations, inasmuch as it rests on the claim that peace-keeping is essentially an anti-escalation device, a reflection of the powers' concern to avoid a major war, and hence situations into which they might be physically and increasingly drawn. It follows that the present improvement in their overall relations takes away a lot of the political impetus behind peace-keeping. For the super-powers are no longer quite so sensitive about the possibility of their rivals' intervention in distant areas, and the chances of such intervention are much less—a development which has been assisted by domestic as well as international factors. Accordingly, the argument runs, the need to put out or isolate ' brush fires ' and to fill ' vacuums ' has been reduced, and with it the prospect of a frequent peace-keeping role for the UN.

The international atmosphere is certainly much less tense than a decade ago, so that a crisis similar to that which occurred in the Congo in 1960 is perhaps unlikely to receive the virtually frantic response which that one obtained. A small but not insignificant pointer in this respect is the almost offhand way in which the Secretary-General received a request from Equatorial Guinea at the end of February 1969 for a UN force to deal with the violations of its sovereignty and independence which were allegedly being perpetrated by the Spanish forces based there. Several cables were sent to this effect, but all they produced was the information that the dispatch of a force would require the authorization of the Security Council, and an offer to send a personal representative to assist in the resolution of the problems which had arisen with Spain. Even allowing for the relative unimportance of the incident, it is unlikely that ten years ago U Thant's predecessor would have reacted so phlegmatically. In part this is no doubt due to the lessened fear of great-power intervention in Africa and consequent escalation. But this does not mean that the UN's earlier peace-keeping efforts were chiefly a response to such apprehensions. They did appear to be present in the Congo crisis—whether well founded or not—and may therefore have influenced the decision to assist in the restoration of law and order. They were not, however, the only motivating factors, and it is much more difficult to see the UN's other operations in this light.

In the case of Suez, for example, there seemed very little chance indeed of physical conflict between the great powers, Khrushchev's advertisement of Soviet rocket power notwithstanding. Rather the UN's action represented a straightforward desire on the part of the vast majority of members to get the aggressors out of Egypt, with the United States to the fore on account of the embarrassment she was caused by the misbehaviour of her NATO allies. Intra-NATO embarrassment was equally if not more pronounced in the Cyprus crisis of 1963–4, which resulted in the dispatch of a UN Force to the island. But for this Greece and Turkey might well have gone to war, with a third NATO member—Britain—literally standing between the lines of fire. The willingness of the UN to assist in the prevention of such a conflict can hardly be ascribed to a concern about its possible impact on East-West relations. The same has to be said regarding the UN's contribution to the resolution of the dispute over West New Guinea, where the war which threatened was between a NATO member and a leading non-aligned state. Other cases in which the UN has played a significant peace-keeping role have been even more remote from great-power politics: disputes between the Lebanon and Syria(1958), the Yemen and Saudi Arabia (1963–4), and India and Pakistan (in Kashmir since 1949 and along the Indo-West Pakistan border in 1965–6). The long Palestinian dispute, in which the UN has played a continuous but fluctuating part, bears rather more directly on the interests of the major powers. But even here it is stretching things to suggest that the UN has been principally moved by a fear of direct great-power involvement, or that this would probably have occurred but for the Organization's peace-keeping efforts. Of course, escalation is always possible in any dispute, and could take place in the most unexpected way. In that sense the UN has helped to guard against a conceivable danger in all these conflicts. But that is a very long way from saying that peace-keeping is primarily an anti-escalation device, which will become less important as the cold war abates.

If it were necessary to identify a single factor which finds general expression in the UN's peace-keeping activities, the choice would fall on the widespread contemporary desire to keep armed conflict between states to a minimum. Exceptions can be found to this trend, particularly with regard to Southern Africa and the Middle East. Note must also be taken of the tendency to interfere in the internal affairs of some states for ideological reasons. But it can be argued that, by and large, the outbreak of hostilities between two established states is regarded as a bad thing, which calls for an early cease-fire and, if possible, a resolution of the underlying problems. The achievement of these goals often requires the services of an impartial intermediary, and it is in this way that the UN has come into its own as a peace-keeping agency.

Moreover, there is no reason to suppose that further action of this kind will be substantively hindered by the lack of advance planning, or, indeed, by the suspicious attitude of France and the Soviet Union which is largely reflected in that lack. It would from many points of view be much more satisfactory if the UN could move smoothly into peace-keeping gear when called upon to do so, knowing where it could find the necessary men, money, and equipment. The efficiency with which the logistical requirements of the Cyprus Force have been provided, thanks to the presence on the island of a British military base, is a welcome contrast with this aspect of other UN operations. But the absence of efficiency, while irritating to those on the spot, is not a crucial failing so far as the UN is concerned. For the nature of peace-keeping is such that the immediate mobilization of resources and split-second timing is not essential. The UN is not moving to repel aggression but in the context of an agreement to stop fighting, or not to start it. Hence if there is some difficulty over finding appropriate troops or transporting their equipment, this is not likely to jeopardize the whole enterprise. Money, of course, needs to be forthcoming, and it would certainly be much easier for the UN if there was a straightforward and assured source, so as to avoid a periodic begging-bowl exercise, such as that which the Cyprus operation requires. But if there are some reasonably wealthy states who feel they have a stake in the launching and maintenance of an operation, it is improbable that it will founder on financial rocks.

What any significant peace-keeping activity does presuppose, however—or at least finds highly desirable—is the approval, in whatever degree of warmth, of the major powers. And here a distinction must be drawn between their attitude towards peace-keeping in the abstract and in particular cases. For although two of them have adopted a consistently discouraging approach towards the idea that the UN should fit itself for peace-keeping operations, they have not vetoed any specific proposals for the mounting of such operations during the last ten years. Nor, so far as is known, have they prevented any formal proposals being made by announcing their opposition in private. Rather, what they have done is to underline their opposition to any course which might conceivably encourage or assist the UN to take action contrary to the wishes of any permanent member of the Security Council. In the case of France this seems to express a principled objection to the idea of international organizations exercising some of the prerogatives which have traditionally been attached to states and states alone. Such bodies, in the French view, need to be kept in their proper subordinate place. Possibly this attitude may undergo some modification during the post-de-Gaulle period. A change in the Soviet position is much less likely, for it is based on a keen consciousness of her minority position in the UN, and on the consequent possibility that attempts might be made to use the Organization in a manner which is hostile to her interests. Even though peace-keeping would not normally touch on issues which were vital to the powers, this is a development which the Soviet Union is most anxious to avoid.

But so far as UN action in crises is concerned, it is reasonable to suppose that, by and large, French and Soviet co-operation will continue. For, with Britain and the United States, they share an interest in international stability and the dampening of conflict, and peace-keeping generally serves this cause. Thus it would not be surprising if the four powers continue to find they have a common mind about the desirable short-term goal in respect of certain international problems, and agree on the use of the UN as the most convenient way of reaching it. Some observers think that this tendency is now so pronounced that it will find early expression in the Peace-keeping Committee in at least some guidelines for future operations, and that formal agreements with the UN regarding stand-by peace-keeping contingents, including some from Eastern-bloc countries, are not to be excluded. Great-power support for specific operations is not dependent on such developments, however, nor is the UN's ability to mount them, and where that support is forthcoming it is exceedingly improbable that the Organization as a whole would be unwilling or unable to meet the wishes of its chief members.

It is unlikely, therefore, that the UN's peace-keeping work has, to all intents and purposes, come to an end. A recent instance, in a minor key, of the Organization's usefulness in this respect is the part which it played in the resolution of Iran's long-standing claim to Bahrain. Presently a British protected state, a question arose regarding its future following the decision of Britain's Labour Government to withdraw from the Persian Gulf in 1971. Informed observers were of the view that there was very little desire in Bahrain to join Iran, and it proved that Iran was prepared to take a conciliatory line. However, she was unwilling simply to renounce her case or to let it go by default. What was needed, therefore, was some means by which Iran could abandon her claim without loss of face, and early in 1969 the Shah said that he would accept any expression of the will of the Bahrainis about their future which world opinion would recognize as genuine. This clearly pointed to the UN as the ratifying device and also, to avoid doubts about what was being presented for ratification, as the investigatory organ, and during the next twelve months a number of references were made to the possibility of it being used for these purposes.

The Shaikh of Bahrain indicated his agreement, in principle, to the idea, but reacted less warmly to the Iranian suggestion that what the UN should be asked to do was to conduct a plebiscite: that form of popular consultation was deemed unsuitable for the Shaikh's domain. However, this problem was sorted out and at the end of March 1970 the UN Secretary-General was able to announce that at the request of Britain and Iran he was sending a personal representative to Bahrain to ascertain the wishes of the inhabitants regarding their future, Iran promising to accept his report provided it was endorsed by the Security Council. After little more than a month the representative declared that the overwhelming majority of the people sought full independence, and on 11 May the Security Council unanimously passed an approving resolution jointly sponsored by Britain and Iran. Congratulatory speeches followed. A month later it emerged that the UN's journey may not have been really necessary, for the Conservative Party came to power in Britain, raising a doubt as to whether there would, after all, be a British withdrawal from the Gulf. None the less, Iran's waiver of her claim cannot but be accounted as making some contribution towards stability in this sensitive region, for it both extinguishes a potent source of dispute and removes one obstacle in the way of the firm establishment of the Union of Arab Emirates, which is haltingly emerging along the western shore of the Gulf. In the achievement of this result the UN undoubtedly deserves credit for its subordinate but valuable patching-up activity.

An area which is often cited as one in which the UN could figure significantly is the Middle East, as both American and Soviet ideas about a settlement appear to include provision for, or at least not to exclude the possibility of, the re-establishment of a UN force to watch over borders and strategic points and perhaps also demilitarized zones. But the expectation that peace-keeping will continue does not depend on an ability to identify areas or issues in which the UN might well become involved. Rather it turns on the assumption that international conflict will persist, and that sometimes there will be a wish to associate the UN with its suspension or settlement on account of the Organization's ability to play a variety of appropriate roles.

This is not to say that the UN will often be called upon to take peace-keeping action. As in the past, the major powers will undoubtedly want to keep their disputes with each other exclusively in their own hands, and the two super-powers will in all probability remain very sensitive to suggestions that the Organization's personnel should operate in Eastern Europe or Latin America. Communist China, too, will almost surely be hostile to the UN's involvement near her borders for as long as she is not given the Chinese seat in the Security Council, and perhaps even after she has obtained it. Lesser states who feel in danger may be expected to maintain their preference for a guarantee from a powerful friend rather than a small non-fighting UN force. Nor is there any reason to anticipate that regional agencies, especially the Organization of African Unity, will be less anxious than formerly to ensure that disputes among their members are kept away from the UN. Thus it must not be supposed that there will be a wide range of opportunities for UN action. Suitable crises may in fact be few. But a long gap between one peace-keeping operation and another does not mean that the international society is no longer capable of producing the kind of issue which is thought to call for UN treatment, nor that when such an issue does arise the UN will have atrophied from disuse, or will be by-passed on this ground. States tend to exhibit a pragmatic frame of mind, and where there is a need for an impartial and extra-regional third party the UN may be expected to figure prominently on the short list, especially where relatively large-scale activity is required, such as the mobilization of a military force.

The contribution which UN peace-keeping activity can make towards security, however, is limited. It is very well illustrated by the three operations which, as of the end of June 1970, are under way. In Kashmir the UN's small group of military observers are assisting in the maintenance of quiet along the cease-fire line. It is the current wish of both India and Pakistan that there should be no trouble in this quarter, and the UN is able to contribute towards the achievement of this goal by being on hand to deal with any incidents which arise. But if either party should change its policy, and opt for physical conflict, the military observers would be unable to do anything about it— as was seen in the events of 1965. Likewise in Cyprus, the UN Force is able to operate successfully because it does so within a favourable political context. The two Cypriot communities, one of them represented by the country's Government, and the two interested outsiders—Greece and Turkey—are all currently anxious to avoid a repetition of the events of Christmas 1963, which led first to British intervention and then to the UN's assumption of the interpository role. Thus although potentially dangerous inter-communal incidents continue to arise, the UN is able to keep them in check and to help in the reduction of local tension. If, however, either of the communities wanted a show-down, the situation would be beyond the UN's prophylactic capabilities.

As an instance of this kind of development the UN's third contemporary operation may be cited, which involves the presence of military observers along two of the cease-fire lines which Israel set up in 1967 at the end of the Six-Day War: those with Syria and the UAR. The observers' chief task is to persuade local commanders to put an early end to any firing which breaks out, and to assist in the settlement of other incidents —a continuation of the function which their predecessors performed, with a fair amount of success, along the armistice lines which were established around Israel in 1949. But that earlier success was dependent on the willingness of the parties to maintain relative outward calm. This situation held in respect of the Israeli-Syrian cease-fire line until the early months of 1970, for while Syria was virulent in her denunciation of Israel and was the only Arab state which would not even discuss a possible settlement with the UN Mediator, she refused to take significant action against Israel or to let the Arab guerrilla movement operate from her soil. No doubt her non-provocative attitude was closely related to the fact that since the 1967 war Israeli forces have been favourably poised only forty miles from Damascus. Then, however, Syria's military activity began to increase, bringing a substantial Israeli reply at the beginning of April 1970 which led to an air battle and an artillery duel along the whole of the thirty-mile cease-fire line.

Early in June serious fighting broke out again, and further incidents were followed at the end of the month by a three-day period of very fierce exchanges, which included armoured incursions across the cease-fire line. Some observers saw Syria's increased belligerence as chiefly a response to the latest American peace proposals, both to mark her displeasure at their reported failure to mention an Israeli withdrawal from the strategically important area of Syria which she had held since the Six-Day War, and to underline Syria's general policy of intransigence. If this analysis is correct it does not necessarily presage a permanent worsening of the position in this sector, and the UN observers could continue to play a useful prophylactic role, at least intermittently. They would be unable to do so, however, if an alternative analysis proves more accurate: that June's developments mark the opening of a second regular Arab-Israel front, said to have been urged on Syria by President Nasser to make things easier for his country along the Suez Canal—the so-called cease-fire line between Israel and the UAR.

There the situation had begun to deteriorate towards the end of 1968, and the parties soon developed a pattern of very frequent firing on a substantial scale. So much so that, in April 1969, in what was to be the first of a number of similar statements, the UN Secretary-General declared that the cease-fire in the Canal sector had become almost totally ineffective. His words were underlined in July of that year when Israel began to attack Egyptian positions from the air in missions of increasing depth. In these circumstances there is little of value that the observers along the Canal can do. Doubtless they are kept there chiefly to maintain the UN's presence in an area where the Organization may in future be able once again to serve a useful purpose, but which would probably be much more difficult of access if an operation had to be set up from scratch.

What the UN can do in the peace-keeping field, therefore, is to help disputants to implement their desire for peace or quiet. It cannot force them to any such disposition, or keep them in that frame of mind. But if they are anxious for either of these things, the UN can provide them with valuable, and perhaps essential assistance. India and Pakistan, for example, could probably avoid conflict in Kashmir without a UN operation, for the local forces are well disciplined and favourably disposed towards the pacific policies of their Governments. But calm is maintained a good deal more easily and surely on account of the presence of UN observers. Likewise, if Egypt and Israel had put their minds to it, they might, from 1957 onwards, have been able to prevent serious incidents, and the consequent possibility of war, without the help of an interpository UN Force. There is little doubt, however, that the Force vastly facilitated the achievement of this goal. And in the case of Cyprus since 1964 there seems every likelihood that but for the UN Force there would have been serious fighting between the two communities, resulting first in Turkish and then in Greek intervention.

All this falls far short of those ' effective collective measures for the prevention and removal of threats to the peace ' of which the Charter speaks. But sometimes it is difficult for individual governments to act with resolve and effect even against internal threats to their authority. It is therefore hardly to be expected that in the present international society virtually all states will regularly combine their forces in a common cause. What they have been able to do during the UN's life is occasionally to authorize the Organization to help in the damping down or snuffing out of armed conflict. Such peace-keeping operations are of secondary rather than primary importance, inasmuch as they are dependent on a prior willingness to move in a pacific direction. But the ability of the parties to make a move of this kind may be materially assisted by and may perhaps actually turn upon an impartial third party, such as the UN, involving itself in the peace-making or peace-preserving process. What the UN offers, therefore, is a marginal contribution towards security, an increment which in itself is small but which may be invested by the circumstances of the specific case with considerable and perhaps crucial significance. The disputes in which the UN is able to play this part are unlikely to bear directly on peace and war among the super-powers. But in respect of some other issues there is no reason to expect that the Organization's marginal security role will be any less valuable and valued during the 1970s than it has been in the past.

Suggestions for Further Reading

Bloomfield, Lincoln P. & others. *International military forces*. Boston, Little, Brown, 1964.

Burns, E. L. M. *Between Arab and Israeli*. London, Harrap, 1962.

Claude, Inis L. Jr. *The changing United Nations*. New York, Random House, 1967.

—— The United Nations and the use of force. *International Conciliation*, March 1961.

Cox, Arthur M. *Prospects for peacekeeping*. Washington DC, Brookings, 1967.

Ditchley Foundation. *The role of force in international order and United Nations peace-keeping*. By Alan James (Rapporteur). 1969.

Finkelstein, Marina S. & Lawrence S., eds. *Collective security*. San Francisco, Chandler, 1966.

Goodrich, Leland M. *Korea: a study of US policy in the United Nations*. New York, Council on Foreign Relations, 1956.

Harbottle, Michael. *The impartial soldier*. London, Oxford University Press for RIIA, 1970.

Horn, Carl von. *Soldiering for peace*. London, Cassell, 1966.

James, Alan. *The politics of peace-keeping*. London, Chatto, 1969.

Larus, Joel, ed. *From collective security to preventive diplomacy*. New York, Wiley, 1965.

O'Brien, Conor Cruise. *To Katanga and back*. London, Hutchinson, 1962.

Russell, Ruth B. *The United Nations and United States security policy*. Washington, DC, Brookings, 1968.

—— *United Nations experience with military forces*. Washington, DC, Brookings, 1964.

Stoessinger, John G. *The United Nations and the superpowers*. New York, Random House, 1965.

Young, Oran R. *Trends in international peace-keeping*. Princeton, Center for International Studies, 1966.

4

PROBLEMS OF SECURITY IN EUROPE

Peter Nailor

As the war in Europe came to an end in the spring of 1945, the inconsistencies and compromises which were inherent in the co-operation between the Western allies and the Soviet Union became more obvious. Such unity as they had achieved was related only to the objective of defeating Germany; what should happen when Japan alone remained to be dealt with had been discussed, but by no means decided. Yet by May 1945 much had been done to deal with immediate problems that would have to be dealt with at the end of hostilities; occupation areas had, in very general terms, been sorted out, and some attempt had been made to deal with the practical as well as the theoretical implications of reparations and relief. Most impressive of all, the United Nations Organization was under way, with the United States and the Soviet Union both firmly committed to participate in its structure. It seemed as though the 1919–21 lessons of peace-making had not merely been learned but were being applied.

Nevertheless it was already clear that the plans embodied no fundamental agreement about the nature of the peace settlement in Europe, or even about the way in which the decisions should be put into effect—as the organization and constitution of a government for liberated Poland was to demonstrate so quickly. Robert Hunter has recently suggested that nothing existed immediately after the end of the Second World War that made what we now call the cold war inevitable: ' the problems of European security, whether viewed from the East or the West, were at first related, not to military matters, but rather to matters of political organization and stability, as well as to pressing matters of economic recovery and strength'.[1] Yet the absence of agreement between the principal protagonists

[1] *Security in Europe* (London, 1969).

in the war against Germany about what should be the nature of the settlement with their defeated adversary was a significant indication of the temporary nature of their wartime co-operation. Both East and West plainly recognized the importance of a settlement in Germany as the basis of security for Europe and in Europe, but their inability to agree among themselves how it might be accomplished could hardly fail to imply an underlying hostility—or at least incompatibility—between them; and given the ways in which international disagreement can be expressed, and the earlier relationship between the Western powers and the Soviet Union, a military dimension was always likely to be added to the situation.

The military dimension has now come to be the most enduring element in the structuring of the division between the two halves of Europe. On the Western side, the North Atlantic Treaty Organization, first from its function and then from its institutional strength, has become a symbol of the unity of purpose which was created in the late 1940s and early 1950s under the threat of Soviet expansionism. Whether that threat was well perceived can fruitfully now be a matter for academic debate,[2] but at the time the danger seemed real enough and the determination to handle it firmly and early owed a great deal to lessons deduced from the omissions and failures of the political leaders of the 1930s. Both East and West in fact became sufficiently sure that they could descry prospective adversaries to replace the ogre of Nazi Germany for the late 1940s to become a period of marked international confusion, elevated indeed to the level of intense diplomatic activity. The benefit which Western Europe won out of the mêlée was the progressive commitment of the United States militarily, as well as economically and politically, to its support. The rebuilding of the damaged economies, and the re-establishment of stable systems of government on the Continent, were matters of high priority, and United States assistance was invaluable. Militarily, it was indispensable, as the lines of the division between East and West hardened and the scope of disagreements became more openly defined. The benefit which the Soviet Union gained was

[2] Not least because it can help to modify the folk-memories upon which institutions, including governmental bodies, erroneously come to rely.

the consolidation of her position in Eastern Europe, which she believed to be necessary for her own security, as a *cordon sanitaire*. The coup d'état in Czechoslovakia in February–March 1948 marked a high point in this consolidation, and was one of the principal causes making the implicit adversary relationship with the West explicit.

The German Problem

The major cause of disagreement, and the central problem of peace-making, remained how to handle and what to do with defeated Germany. It was not the only problem to be settled in Europe, but it was fundamental. Not only had Germany been the prime enemy—for the second time in the lives of those who were called upon to deal with the situation—but all the major allies had armies in the country, able to dispute the prize which lay, prostrate, between them. Japan was not of the same global importance. Europe, where both world wars had broken out, in diplomatic if not in power cosmology still had a claim to be considered the centre of the universe. At the very broadest level, the Allies all still shared a common aim: to ensure that a Germany dominating *Mitteleuropa* could never again set the world by the ears. How this was to be achieved was a problem on which, as peace approached, the Allies proved to have widely different viewpoints. Initially, the Soviet Union and France had more in common in their attitudes, and were at one end of the spectrum with deeply-felt memories of the brutality of the German occupation of their territory; the United States was inclined more to dust off rather than shake down the bully-boy. Britain appreciated early on that the active involvement of the United States was required to achieve a settlement which could provide a defence against both German revanchist and Soviet expansionist dangers. The zones into which Germany had been split for occupation purposes had no particular validity in logic, and a number of drawbacks in practice (of which the isolated position of Berlin was only the most notable). They gave no guide about what the eventual nature of a German state or states might be, or whether the zones should be durable: the measure of agreement which was achieved at, and immediately after, the Potsdam Conference did not last sufficiently long to provide a basis for consistent policies in the separate zones. The inefficiency and expense of maintaining the United States and British zones as separate entities led in 1947 to 'Bizonia', and eventually to the combination of all three Western areas into what is now West Germany. The Soviet Union's policy was to exact what reparations she could: to compensate Poland with German territory for the loss of her Eastern provinces; to establish a Communist polity in the Soviet-occupied zone, both for its own sake and against the day when free elections might be held in a reunited Germany and, in general, to use East Germany as part of the buffer-zone of dependent states which would give her space and time against the capitalist onslaught that Stalin expected. More generally in Europe, her aims were to use the territory she had acquired, or could now dominate, and the influence she had gained by her tremendous exertions in the Great Patriotic War, to support her claims to have a dominant role in the settlement of European affairs.

None of these policies, as they evolved, took much account of the susceptibilities of the other major protagonists. Soviet fear of invasion might be exaggerated, but it was real; Western assumptions about the necessity for democratic constitutions in the liberated territories might well be aimed at the basis of Communist theory, but they also stemmed from a genuine concern for freedom and prosperity as well as from some concern to avoid repeating the mistakes of Versailles; American concern to achieve the efficient, mechanistic result might undervalue political sensibilities, but it was humane and effective. There was no protracted attempt to find how such incompatibilities might be overcome and, once the pattern of wartime co-operation had broken down, as it had before the end of 1947, there was no real attempt to discover whether, as between the extremes of the Soviet and United States positions, there was any basis for identifying means whereby a European settlement could be jointly determined. The machinery by which a settlement might be implemented was there; some of the principles on which it might be based were there; but the will to make the settlement was not. Europe was cast into a plaster-of-Potsdam mould; and the more clear it became that there was no common understanding on

Europe as a whole, the more important the strategic hiatus created by the dismemberment of Germany became.

On the military side, the United States' commitment lost nothing of essentiality after Russia broke the United States' monopoly of atomic weapons, and after the Korean War gave wider credence to the theories that Soviet expansionist aims would take a military form. The principles of forward planning and of the prior commitment of resources embodied in the NATO arrangements were accepted as the basic requirements of preparedness in the atomic age. As the prospect of nuclear war became more awful to contemplate, and more likely to affect the homelands of the two principal protagonists, there grew a more lively appreciation of the need to possess a spectrum of conventional power to deal with what one American authority movingly called ' a kick below the nuclear belt ' and, subsequently, of the need for caution in handling crises. On the Eastern side, the Warsaw Pact has never had the same functional utility as NATO in diplomatic or alliance manoeuvring; but it embodies a military potential, particularly at the conventional level, of great strength, alongside which it has been the custom that the capabilities of the NATO forces have had to be measured. How such measurements can be made with tolerable accuracy, and what are the correct deductions to be drawn from theoretical comparisons of effectiveness, has never been satisfactorily resolved by NATO, even with the assistance of quantitative analytical methods.

The issue is of more than abstruse theoretical importance; NATO has to provide forces not only to deter the Warsaw Pact countries from attacking, but also to defend the NATO countries if deterrence should fail. Whether this means providing enough conventional strength to fight, and conceivably win, a conventional war on the 1939–45 model, or whether it would be sufficient to have forces strong enough to hold a Soviet attack for a short period while the processes of nuclear intimidation were brought into play, has never been agreed. Moreover, the wide geographical spread of NATO influences different perceptions of risktaking. A nation that adjoins Soviet-dominated territory, like West Germany, has a different set of priorities from countries like Great Britain, Italy, and most significantly the United

States, which are separated from any immediate threat of Soviet occupation, and might hope to avoid some of the early consequences, at least, of a Soviet attack.

The Proposed European Security Conference

In the aftermath of the Cuban crisis of October 1962 there was a relaxation of tension between East and West which lasted until the summer of 1968. In general, it involved a sharper distinction between the direct relationship of the United States and the Soviet Union at the one level and their relationships with their respective allies at another. The direct relationship was highlighted by the way in which the allies were kept on the sidelines during the Cuban crisis;[3] the dependent relationship was shown on the Western allies' side to be useful both in welcoming the reduced likelihood of conflict between the super-powers and in justifying a declining expenditure on their own security forces. It was assumed that there were ameliorative forces at work in the East as well as in the West; as the strategic power of the Soviet Union grew—and provided super-power *détente* could be maintained—it was surely reasonable, by Western criteria, to expect that the Soviet Union would downgrade the importance of her Eastern European redoubt, and might even outgrow her fear of attack from the West. Soviet foreign policy gave some credence to these hopes in the period of improved relations after the 1955 Geneva Conference and again after the fall of Khrushchev when, as Zbigniew Brzezinski has pointed out,[4] it was more sensitive to the general European mood than Western alliance, and particularly United States, official initiatives at that time. The Soviet Union encouraged the thought that improvements in relations between East and West could move on from increased 'cultural' and economic contacts to wider political issues, and refurbished proposals for a European Security Conference that had originally been mooted in the

---

[3] It is possible to state a case that the reactions of Britain and France to this experience were similar to the ways in which they had reacted in 1956–7, after their joint Suez expedition. General de Gaulle moved away from the American connection and began individual manoeuvring towards both Russia and W. Germany; Macmillan went to Nassau and set about obtaining a deterrent capability based on US hardware.

[4] 'The Framework of East-West Reconciliation', *Foreign Affairs*, Jan. 1968.

Molotov era at the time of the debates about West German independence and rearmament. Some of the Eastern European states, notably Rumania, saw in these proposals a prospect that a reduction of tension between East and West would lead to a diminution of Soviet pressure upon themselves. The attraction that this sort of *démarche* had to the West, even though in detail it might be unacceptable, was that it might enable the two, highly armed, military blocs to move towards a system of mutual guarantees, saving men and money for everybody, and dismantling something at any rate of the apparatus of hostility. It would safeguard the *status quo* while at the same time allowing rather more freedom for the exercise of political influence.

Safeguarding the *status quo*, however, focused attention once again upon the existence of two German states, but the Soviet approach ' simply disregards the fact that the unsolved legacies of the Second World War cannot be resolved by a fiat that transforms them miraculously into a generally accepted and enduring settlement '.[5] The first major proposal for a European Security Conference in the 1960s was made by the Warsaw Pact Consultative Committee in January 1965, after a speech by the Polish foreign minister to the UN General Assembly. It was renewed in the following year by Brezhnev at the Communist Party Congress in Moscow, in March 1966, though in less specific terms. Rapacki and Gomulka had suggested an atom-free zone in Central Europe, a freeze on nuclear weapon armouries, a treaty of non-aggression between NATO and the Warsaw Pact, and a German settlement based upon the international recognition of the two German states. Brezhnev cast his suggestions in terms more likely to appeal to general European sentiment, and more openly aimed at the debates and dissensions which were then preoccupying NATO.

The proposals were revamped in Bucharest in July 1966 and at Karlovy Vary in April 1967, in ways which indicated that considerable debate was taking place about the utility of the proposals in relation to problems within Eastern Europe as well as in regard to the Eastern bloc's relations with the West. Gromyko referred to the need to convene a European Security Conference when he spoke at the UN in October 1968 in the

[5] Ibid.

aftermath of the invasion of Czechoslovakia; but the next major restatement of the proposals came in March 1969, just in time to be considered at the 20th anniversary meeting of NATO. The proposals on this occasion were couched in fairly specific terms, and were extended to include anti-pollution co-operation as well as political, economic, and cultural ties. The question of whether the United States should participate was not dealt with explicitly. The priority given to the strengthening of the position of the Berlin-Pankow regime was very clear, and the general note was one of requiring the acceptance of the existing *status quo* as a precondition for a conference.

But successive refinements of the Soviet proposals have not been able to mask the issue of the two Germanies, which has recently been restated in these terms:

It is imperative to secure the inviolability of existing frontiers in Europe, in particular the frontiers along the Oder–Neisse and the frontier between the Federal Republic of Germany and the German Democratic Republic, and to work for international legal recognition of the German Democratic Republic, for preventing West Germany from securing atomic weapons in any form, for renunciation by the Federal Republic of Germany of her claim to represent the whole of Germany, the recognition of West Berlin as a separate political entity, the recognition that the Munich *Diktat* was invalid from the very outset, and the banning of all neo-Nazi organizations.[6]

The ability of West Germany, and of the Western allies as a group, to envisage meeting this set of conditions is strictly limited, even assuming that there would be unanimity about the concessions that should be made. There might well be, as the initiatives by Chancellor Brandt have shown that there could be, a reconciliation of the Federal Republic to the continued existence of an East German state. But this could solve no problems in itself, however useful it might be as a symbolic acceptance of the division of Germany, and the allies of both Germanies have interests which have to be taken into account. It would be a useful start, and perhaps an essential first step, but not much more. It would have to be balanced, on the Soviet side, by some positive indications that genuine negotiations

---

[6] 'Basic Document' adopted by the Moscow Conference, July 1969, quoted by M. D. Shulman, 'A European Security Conference', *Europa-Archiv*, Folge 19/1969, reprinted in *Survival*, Dec. 1969.

would follow, and that the conditions were not ends in them-selves.[7]

The chance of developing something more, a wider agreement of the type postulated in the heyday of *détente*, was seriously undermined by the Warsaw Pact invasion of Czechoslovakia in August 1968. Czechoslovakia, of course, had something of a touchstone quality for the Westerners, who recalled not only 1948 but 1938 as well. The invasion made no major change in the military balance of power in Europe, but it did quash any assumption that the Soviet Union was prepared to consider any major variations in her relationship with the countries of Eastern Europe, especially those in the strategically sensitive 'northern tier'. It was not merely Czechoslovakia's political loyalty which was at stake, or the pace at which reform was being carried out, but ideological conformity. The invasion itself, and more especially the thoroughness with which the reformers were subsequently displaced, gave credence to the supposition that the Soviet Union acted in order to prevent the possibility that revisionism in Czechoslovakia, and perhaps in Poland as well, would spread, to undermine the authority of the Communist system in Eastern Europe and might even infect the Soviet Union itself, though this is more conjectural. Russia was sufficiently disturbed to risk her standing as a world power in order to avert this local danger; and was suffi-ciently concerned with the consequences of this risk to devote a great deal of effort in the succeeding months to an attempt to rehabilitate herself.

The effort was in part successful. Although there was a great deal of concern in Western Europe (and some evidence of concern in Eastern Europe as well) at the invasion of Czecho-slovakia, it did not materially affect the impulse to find a more normal basis of relations with the Soviet Union and Eastern Europe (more normal, that is, than the conditions of the earlier periods in the cold war had permitted), but making due allow-ance for the need to offset the contiguity of the Soviet Union by the involvement of the United States. That was one factor which did not alter; but the invasion of Czechoslovakia did

[7] See K. E. Birnbaum, 'Ways Towards European Security', *Europa-Archiv*, Folge 7/1968, reprinted in *Survival*, June 1968.

materially affect the time-scale within which major alterations in the existing pattern of arrangements could realistically be envisaged. It hardened the relationships between East and West again and demonstrated starkly how far Europe was from returning to the Gaullist ideal of *Europe des États*, a multilateral system of international relations. The rejuvenation of NATO and the closer relationship of France to the rest of the Western allies was only a partial compensation, which cannot effectively offset the need to go back to first principles and establish what are the conditions and arguments that both East and West can use in discussing the place and future of the two halves of Europe. In this respect the proposals for a European Security Conference are suspect, since they have been regarded in the past by NATO as being aimed primarily at either the parties to dissension within the alliance (as in 1954–5 and 1965–6) or at interests which want to play down particular situations of stress or more open hostility between the blocs (as in October 1968).

How long the rejuvenation of NATO will persist, and how far France will be prepared to go in abandoning the form as well as the content of Gaullist policy remains to be seen, and will depend in part upon the assumptions which the various parties make about the stability of American-Soviet relationships. Militarily, France seems to be moving nearer to NATO concepts of strategy,[8] but this is unlikely to mean that she would be prepared to return to participation in the integrated structure of NATO. It is by no means certain that the other European members would willingly accept a loosening of this structure, not least because it might be taken, symbolically, as a loosening of alliance cohesion, unless the reorganization was one which the United States approved and to which she was a party. It is difficult to see how this could take place, except in the context of a general rearrangement of security relationships.

The crucial nature of the German problem, and its long standing, should not obscure the existence of other problem areas. The Central European front has exercised a mesmerism for NATO experts, because that is where the major allied forces are stationed, that is where the *Bundeswehr* in particular is

---

[8] See the article by Gen. Fourquet in *Revue de Défense Nationale,* May 1969.

I

concentrated, and that is where the most sophisticated pro-
fessional military problems are thought most likely to arise.[9]
It is arguable however that other areas—either because they
are less well policed, as in the case of the Northern flank, or
inherently more volatile, as in the case of the South-eastern
flank—are most likely to become areas in which the potential
for military clashes is greater. There is plenty of tinder in
southern Europe and the eastern basin of the Mediterranean,
where the Soviet Union has developed an effective intervention
capability and a solid set of neo-imperialist liabilities in the
Arab world which make the Arab-Israeli struggle of more direct
interest to Europe than the intractable nature of the struggle
itself. Cyprus still remains a source of dispute between Greece
and Turkey; Greece is still formally at war with Albania, and
there are various territorial and ethnic disputes between the
Soviet Union and Rumania, Hungary and Rumania, Bulgaria
and Yugoslavia, some of which go back to the classical days of the
nineteenth-century Balkan problem. The sources of conflict
between Italy and Austria, and Britain and Spain can perhaps
be dismissed lightly in comparison. Some of these issues have
an intrinsic importance, which offers some danger that the
heat they might generate would spread elsewhere in Europe;
in this connection the exposed position of the Western allies in
Berlin is always a situation that has to be carefully considered,
because it is so easy to exploit. Even if all these possibilities
for conflict remain hypothetical, however, they do serve to
emphasize that the recognition by Bonn of the Berlin–Pankow
regime cannot be the end of the search for a European security
system that embraces Europe as a whole—even though it may
be thought to be a useful beginning.

Super-power détente

Pierre Hassner has observed wryly that 'the search for a
European security system has nothing to do with any direct
search for security '[10] and it seems incontestable that the efforts

[9] It therefore also allows for the greater display of analytical legerdemain, and
offers the prospects of greatest budgetary saving—and, for the United States
and Britain, a saving of foreign currency.

[10] *Change and Security in Europe*, pt. I: *The Background* (London, iss, Feb. 1968),
p. 4.

and expenditures of the last twenty-five years have given to the European continent a measure of security which it would be foolish to give up lightly.[11] Nevertheless, what may be evident at the military level appears not to be so tolerable at the political and economic levels, and the search for improvement has therefore come to be concentrated upon the paradoxical need for finding a way to move forward in political terms without backsliding in any other way. It is in this context that the achievements of the past threaten to become straitjackets, not least because any discussion of the political objectives which should be aimed for soon reveals that there is still no common viewpoint between East and West on the problems held over from the delayed peace settlement. On the one hand, it ought to be possible to discuss some of them in a more objective way, and with more clearly perceived interests, after the passage of so long a time; but, on the other hand, the passage of time has created new institutions (for example, the two Germanies) and new interests. Organizations that were set up to serve specific purposes have been able to acquire that powerful and regenerative institutional inertia that political (and academic) bureaucrats alike find so absorbing. This distorting patina is nowhere likely to have a more important influence than in the attitude of the United States and the Soviet Union, whose relationships to Europe and to each other have altered since the cold-war postures were first struck.

The emergence of the Soviet Union as a world power—rather than as a dominant regional power—owes something to the readiness of the United States to treat her in the postwar period as a world-wide adversary. In so far as this relationship was first focused in Europe and has been most successfully sustained there, the readiness (if it really does exist) of the United States' European allies to alter the security relationship so expensively built up may become a source of friction with the United States. American interests in Europe have not changed very

[11] They have also given Europe a measure of stability. The question now becomes whether changes can be induced to meet new needs and new situations, or whether stability means stagnation. In the latter event changes become more difficult, and might even give rise to *internal* threats to security, of a significantly different order than the majority of those discussed in this paper.

much over the years though the priorities given to them have varied; Europe is still an important weight in the scales, in terms both of real assets and of the containment of the Soviet Union. United States policy-makers have so far been less willing than their European colleagues to accept the thesis that Soviet intentions no longer extend to a military threat to Western Europe, and they have endeavoured to maintain a high level of military preparedness at some cost to the cohesion of the Western alliance. Yet although a willingness to consider new—and less expensive—ways of securing their interests may now be becoming more marked, there is still room to doubt the readiness of the United States to move towards a new set of arrangements with her allies in order ultimately to achieve a new balance with her main adversary in this crucial area. The stability of any relationship between power blocs depends more heavily now than formerly on the stability of the military balance between them; at the same time there are new constraints upon the use or threat of force between nuclear powers either to maintain or alter the equilibrium. This may lead the United States to conclude that the process of moving from one position of equilibrium to another, and hopefully better, position may either be too uncertain to attempt at all, or should only be attempted by way of the direct relationship with the Soviet Union. A reasonable deduction from this might be that if the movement is to take place in the alliance framework at all—which is a third possible course—it will depend upon the European components developing objectives and methods that are persuasive and reasonable enough to be compelling.

On the Soviet side, there are signs that her priorities vis-à-vis Western Europe are shifting; the new factors are specifically the emergence of a direct relationship with the United States and the growth of concern over China, but there are others as well, like the requirement to strike a new balance of relationships with her Eastern European protégés and, conceivably, some economic fears about the rising costs of being a super-power. The importance of Western Europe in the Soviet scheme of things has probably declined; but any overt process of adjustment, let alone fundamental change, remains a matter of very great importance, both internally and to the Soviet position as the principal protagonist and self-appointed guardian of Eastern European interests. The relative importance of the respective European components in the two blocs is not identical; the different influences of geography—especially of contiguity—ideology, and history all make for asymmetry. On the United States side, involvements of honour and, to a certain extent, of prosperity, as well as the pride of place of NATO in the postwar pattern of containment, go a long way towards offsetting the physical separation of the American and European components of the Atlantic Alliance. Strategically Europe is still an important glacis for both the super-powers; they face each other there in a particularly involved way and their position marks a high point in their developing global relationship in spite of the relative unwillingness of the European satrapies to contribute to their separate global interests. In strictly military terms, the Soviet Union has no special reason for feeling insecure in Europe; this is the central reason for any shift of priority that has already occurred. But her aims are still construed in the general context of maintaining the cohesion of Eastern Europe, of defusing relations with the West generally, of developing mutually beneficial relations in commercial terms; and of working for the eventual advance of Communism.

There, then, are some issues which both super-powers have in common, and there may be some others shared by their dependants. However, two problems stand out as being pervasive: the first is that the probability of war in Europe is generally conceded to be low, the second that of the future place of Germany.

Hassner has pointed out [12] that the diminished fears of aggression and then of accidental war—' the victory of " intentions " over " capabilities " '—have had the consequence of lifting the security concerns of the Soviet Union and the United States to the bilateral strategic level, and of giving rise to doubts about the size and utility of the military investment in Europe. The feeling of security reinforces the power of the *status quo*; but conversely, and more constructively, could be used as a basis for developing ' *status quo plus* '.

[12] *Change and Security*, pt. 1, p. 5.

The belief that the present system is neither permanent nor to be disposed of in the near future at the conference table, and hence has the perspective of a long-range goal to be reached in distinct stages, is the most elegant way out of our double inability to accept the *status quo* and to overthrow it. It does raise, however, the same questions as any other policy which includes the time element as a basic ingredient (like negotiating from strength): it assumes, first, that time works in the desired direction and, second, that one will be able to put it to good use. In the present case, this means both that at least some of the long-range trends in Europe work against the *status quo*, and that the will and the ability exist to exploit, as they arise, the opportunities they will offer.[13]

In general terms, it is possible to see some evidence which supports both these contentions; one need not, for example, be totally pessimistic about the capacity of the political figures of the First Television Generation. Whether shorter-term impulses may not lie awkwardly with longer-term trends is more open to doubt; in particular whether the ' unravelling ' of NATO which developed in the 1960s will not recur and effectively preclude any need for the Soviet Union to negotiate seriously about, for example, the mutual reduction of force levels in Central Europe.

The situation of East Germany exemplifies the artificial nature of some of the complications arising from the unsettled problem of Germany. Two Germanies exist, and the Western allies are still, in form at any rate, committed to achieve their reunification. The Soviet Union recognizes both Bonn and Berlin–Pankow; the West has an increasing interest in the commercial prosperity of East Germany but does not formally recognize her political existence, and can hardly move very far until West Germany herself moves in such a direction. Conversely, any West German initiative that does not take account of the susceptibilities of her Western allies as well as of the fears of her Eastern neighbours will be viewed with some disquiet and must create great difficulties for West German political leaders who wish to come to grips with the realities of the situation of their state, both in external and in internal political relationships. Although there seems to be a marked

[13] Ibid., p. 7.

public willingness within West Germany to accept the division of Germany as a fact which has to be acknowledged, the spectre of what a united Germany could mean in terms of space, force, and resources still arouses emotions, in the West as well as in the East, and one of the chief reasons for American involvement on the ground in Europe is to provide a guarantee that West German policy will be developed within a generally acceptable framework and in an alliance context. ' The United States remains the primary West European power charged with providing security against Germany as well as against the Soviet Union, and has had its role emphasized by the departure of de Gaulle '.[14]

Given, therefore, that the invasion of Czechoslovakia has affected the impetus, but not the impulse, towards ending, in some fashion, the division imposed on Europe a quarter of a century ago, how is change to be effected? There seems no compelling case—and very little evidence of any major manifestations of political will—to dismantle the structures that have evolved over the years unless something more generally satisfactory is to result. In particular, the realities of the central balance between the United States and the Soviet Union preclude any ' private deal ' between the European states themselves. How a better and more stable relationship between the European nations can be achieved, and be reconciled with their connexions with the super-powers, is the principal issue which has to be tackled in dealing with security from external threats;[15] and it can hardly be limited to the question of the directly military aspects of security. What sort of Europe is it going to be that needs to be more secure?

In terms of theory, there are a number of principles on which proposals for change could be based: first, that Europe could become unified, federated, or insulated from direct super-power entanglement by a series of overlapping guarantees, centred on the two Germanies and perhaps modelled on the Locarno settlement; second, that a bipolar organization, based upon the present division, might be developed as a first aim; or,

---

[14] Hunter, *Security in Europe*, ch. 6.

[15] Hassner, *Change and Security in Europe*, pt. 2: *In Search of a System* (July 1968).

third, that one or other or both of the super-powers should disengage from European involvement.[16]

Hassner argues that

the only way to increase independence without diminution of security lies neither in the adoption of a position of passive neutrality, nor of active non-alignment between two monolithic alliances, nor in the replacing of them altogether by a system of flexible balance of power and of shifting alignments, but in making the alignments within the existing groups less automatic and exclusive.[17]

In practice, however, there is little likelihood that any eventual goal can be agreed upon at an early stage, or that the movement towards it can be stable or uniform; the prospects for progress still have to be measured by decades rather than by single years. Diplomacy has an unfortunate resemblance to some aspects of the game of Snakes and Ladders, even when the dice are not loaded; and in the nature of the game, there are likely to be gains and losses. The minimum political requirement is that both players—assuming that there are only two—have a reasonably clear, and agreed, view about what the nature of the game is. Only then will it be feasible for both of them and the onlookers to perceive whether the gains and losses are incidental, or fundamental. To this extent, a consideration of the theoretical possibilities is an essential part of the by-play; and for such a purpose the ruminations of non-officials are a desirable stimulus to governments. In so highly structured and institutionalized a setting as Europe has come to be, it is difficult for governments—and more difficult for international bodies— to speculate freely about postulated alternatives to the modest course of action which is all that a national consensus, imagined or real, or an alliance viewpoint, contrived or imposed, will allow them to acknowledge publicly as a desirable aim. It is almost impossible for them to license unorthodoxy unless they have the resources both to promote it, and then to identify it as unorthodox. On the Western side, the United States has done this extensively in defence and in international relations; British, French, and German efforts have been more modest and have owed much less to direct government support and encouragement.

[16] See A. Buchan, ed., *Europe's Future, Europe's Choices* (London, 1969), for a discussion of some of the major possibilities.

[17] *Change & Security*, pt. 2, p. 17.

In part, European speculation has been focused on the possible variations in the attitude and role of the United States. Opinions have been voiced freely, for rather more than fifteen years, on the willingness, in the event, of the United States to use nuclear weapons on its NATO allies' behalf; and at some stage in their respective developments, though not to the same extent, the British and French national nuclear forces have been based upon the supposition that they might either need to be used alone or as a ' trigger ' mechanism to involve the United States. Speculation about the use of nuclear weapons is, thankfully, an area where theoretical alternatives are the only analytical tools we have, since no substantial body of experience exists. Nevertheless, the theoreticians have forced the decision-makers to come to terms with the jargon, and to deal with the flow of ideas which, because they are designed for the public domain, have been presented with a basis of argument and logic not always necessary in official policy documents which have to meet practical limitations, like being developed from precedent and being equally useful for the demands of today, of tomorrow, and of the budget.

In a sense, however, the theoreticians have been too successful in creating a language and applying a logic which enables nuclear horrifics to be rationally discussed. The rationality has—partly because of its logical elegance—been confused with political likelihood and, having been assimilated by policy-makers seeking a conceptual framework to enshrine their labours, has been given too great a place. Thus a great deal of the discussion about what the United States might or might not do has been misapplied and used as though it were a prediction of what the United States could or should not do. The acceptability of American policy assumptions, designed to meet United States global needs yet expressed to NATO in terms of alliance regional obligations, has fallen away sharply in a situation where Western Europe has at one and the same time outgrown its general dependence upon American economic help and yet feels itself permeated by American economic influence. The allies feel themselves dominated by the continuing requirement to rely upon American military guarantees, but they sense that the alliance has entered a period in which the probability of war is perceptibly less likely to be centred upon Europe. The preoccupation of analysing United States options, and of finding them less and less concerned with European problems, coincided with periods of improved prosperity, of post-imperial nausea, when the euphoria induced by schemes for European integration of varying kinds was fading under the pressure of practical experience. The consequence has been that a more critical evaluation of the American connection coincided with a low point in the ability of the European allies themselves to frame constructive suggestions. General de Gaulle's endeavours to become the European ring-master emphasized both phenomena as well as NATO's capacity on the one hand to cope mechanically with the French decision to withdraw from active participation, and on the other its inability, without a strong United States lead, to determine how the gap between NATO strategy and capability could be overcome. One benefit stemming from the invasion of Czechoslovakia has been the realization by both the United States and the West Europeans, including France, that the Europeans have a larger part to play in creating the framework for any renewed period of *détente* that may lead to a European settlement. The relationship between the circumstances of a super-power *détente*—exemplified by the Strategic Arms Limitation Talks (SALT)—and the necessary conditions for European *détente* still remains uncertain, even though Nixon has made considerable efforts to give reality to his undertaking that the NATO allies will be kept in touch with the development of United States policy towards strategic arms limitation and, implicitly, will be given the opportunity to influence United States negotiating positions.

NATO policy-making is a relatively public affair and the divisions of opinion that have occurred at various times have been widely discussed. The Warsaw Pact has a greater outward appearance of unity and there is little evidence available on which to judge how internal discussions have gone, or even if there have been any major contributions to the strategy of the Pact by the Eastern European allies. The Pact has the advantage of greater geographical cohesion; it derives some practical advantages from the nature of its command structure and from the position of the Soviet Union as the sole source of sophisticated weaponry. It also benefits—though this might conceivably not be the ideal word to use—from the realization that the Soviet Union is in no position to cut herself off; there is therefore a basic identity of interest, at least at the geographical level, between the allies and the Soviet Union about the nature and terms of any European security settlement.

Diversity of opinion outside the specifically military field is more easy to identify, and there are a number of interests in Eastern Europe favouring more effective contacts with the West. East Germany's trade with the West, for example, is already very considerable; she is the leading industrial country of the Eastern bloc, on an output per head basis. Hungary has already, with the Netherlands, proportionately one of the most trade-dependent economies in the world. In similar vein, the Polish foreign minister has acknowledged that the development of economic and trade co-operation always helps to create a climate which facilitates the solution of ' other problems ', i.e. the recognition of the Oder–Neisse frontier, which is at least as important to Poland as to East Germany. It is to be expected that the influence of political and military factors will affect the timing of any co-operative gestures towards the West that might be likely from economic factors alone; but the propensity of trade and commerce to just happen, even in centrally directed economies, may create stronger links and established patterns of contact by a kind of osmosis. Nevertheless, the pace at which politically significant moves take place is likely to be controlled by the Soviet Union, and, since she has consistently construed her security interests in a very broad way in Eastern Europe, the pace will be deliberate. The proposals for a European Security Conference have offered very little of substance so far to the West in realistic terms, even on the assumption that the West has a cohesive and unitary set of identified interests in the issues; the Soviet Union may be impelled to move more constructively—within the framework of these proposals—in political and economic matters. But in the end, it may be that Soviet military security interests will prevail. In this connexion, it is possible that a satisfactory outcome to the SALT discussions with the United States, or the establishment of a more or less permanent super-power dialogue, might lead the Soviet Union to deduce that there was no pressing need to regularize formally the *status quo* in Europe. Although such a position might be unwelcome to the East European allies, it is difficult, given the structure of the Warsaw Pact and COMECON, to see what they could effectively do to alter it in any short compass of time.

Alternatively, if the SALT discussions do not go well, the Soviet Union may be tempted to use overtures to Western Europe as a way of inducing a more conciliatory negotiating position from the United States. In order for this to be successful, she would need something more attractive than she has so far been willing to offer. It seems likely that such offers would be framed in an economic context initially, rather than in directly political or security terms; for the Soviet Union's dilemma in this event would be to produce proposals that were attractive to Western Europe and yet would not be divisive or disruptive in Eastern Europe. Any Soviet moves towards a *démarche* with West Germany would be difficult to place, within such limitations. A more extensive commercial and trade relationship with the West would be a way of achieving a number of desirable ends without conceding any major political points; outlets for goods, opportunities to attract capital as well as Western products and hard currencies, would all be attractive opportunities to East European states. It seems doubtful, however, even if one accepts the Cobdenist assertion that there is a beneficial political spin-off from economic connections, whether the opportunities that could be offered would be sufficiently attractive to West European states to overcome any paucity of concessions at the political level.

Issues facing the Western Alliance

The prospects for the West in developing a policy which suits both Western Europe and the United States, and which stands a useful chance of being negotiable with Eastern Europe and the Soviet Union, depends greatly upon the emergence of a common position between London, Paris, and Bonn. Britain's relations with Europe since the war have shown that although she has wished to play an influential role, a series of countervailing pressures—economic, strategic, and political—have made it difficult for her to pay consistent attention to her European interests. This has led to a detectable confusion and lack of credibility among her neighbours about her long-term intentions. Only in very recent years has a concentration upon her regional position and interests been preferred to the juggling of the three interlocking circles, the United States, the Commonwealth, and Europe, that used to be a persistent metaphor in political exegesis. Nevertheless, the decision once made is unlikely rationally to be reversed, and although Britain will probably remain a country with rather wider horizons than some of her allies, her interests in European security and prosperity now appear to be well enough perceived for full use to be made of her resources.

The case for achieving a close working relationship between Britain, France, and West Germany is partly a simple matter of resources; they are the three largest and most powerful units; for example, without their agreement, there could be no worthwhile system of defence co-operation or any alternative to a virtual United States hegemony in the Atlantic Alliance, nor—given the background to the division in Europe—could either the smaller allies or the Eastern bloc be otherwise satisfied about the place of West Germany in the international system. But there is the countervailing danger that a community of attitude between Britain, France, and Germany has Gaullist overtones, and could all too easily be represented as a tripartite European directorate, giving offence, and no offsetting advantage by comparison with a United States hegemony, to the smaller Western European states. This would be an unfortunate and divisive development, which would hamper the attainment of the broad basis of political agreement that is necessary for any sustained improvements in co-operation, or any more formal system of common endeavour. The whole series of problems that will be involved infers a long time-scale that will call for a marked continuity of resolve, and the welter of European organizations that already exist will have to be constrained within the limits of a broadly conceived programme. The juxtaposition of NATO, WEU, EEC, and EFTA, for example, could easily result in an uncontrollable mêlée of cross-purposes and pressures.

The work of these institutions shows, however, that, with varying degrees of success, it has been possible for European nations to work together for long periods in harmony; each of them indeed has more to record in the way of successes than we sometimes allow ourselves to recall. The search for a new security pattern calls for at least the same degree of resolution, though there seems no reason why it should call for another institution. There is one procedural difficulty, which may be more apparent than real; from many points of view NATO seems the best forum in which to discuss general security issues, from the straight military matter to the mixture of politico-economic matters that many military problems turn out to be. It at least has the widest European membership. Yet NATO transcends European affairs and includes the United States and Canada. Ought they to participate in discussion of specifically European affairs? Ought not the Europeans to try to work out some concepts for themselves? This is a mirror-image within NATO of the issue with which Russia has toyed in developing the successive proposals for a European Security Conference: whether the United States and Canada should be invited to attend. Within NATO, however, there seems to be a greater degree of consistent susceptibility about American feelings among the Europeans than about European feelings among the North Americans. If what the United States has said on many occasions about the Europeans doing more within NATO means anything in terms of general policy, the United States could hardly not welcome an initiative which may assist everyone to achieve a comparable or better assurance of security at a lower price. Yet there is clearly some substance in the European sensitivity to United States feelings; the position of a dominant ally in a multilateral structure is a strong and important one.[18] The United States can hardly in practice avoid being dominant given the disparity between her power base and that of her allies. And the interpolation of the direct super-power relationship between the United States and the Soviet Union adds another complicating factor; so that in the early 1970s we might well see the United States playing three roles in European security at the same time: as the dominant member of the NATO alliance, as the consultant

[18] Cf. La Fontaine: ' La raison du plus fort est toujours la meilleure '.

helping the European group sort its ideas out, and as a protagonist in the SALT discussions with Russia.

There seems little doubt, however, that whether the United States plays an integral part in any discussions, or whether the formative work is done principally in a European forum—which might or might not amount to the ' European identity ' that has been suggested—there is little chance of any substantial progress being made unless at least Great Britain, Germany, and France agree on substantive issues, as well as on procedures, that commend themselves to the rest of Western Europe. What are the prospects?

There are two issues within the European nexus of the Western alliance which constrain the range of possibilities. The first is the relationship of the European allies with the United States. There will be a general disinclination, even though the external military threat to the security of Western Europe from the Soviet Union or Eastern Europe is now thought to be low, to upset the present military relationship. For one thing, no clear alternative to the Soviet-American balance of power is visible, although the sheer disparity between the resources of Russia and the United States and those which any single European nation can now assemble is so dramatic that it must be a cause of continuing political concern in individual relationships. In the second place, the military contribution of the United States is not merely irreplaceable at the nuclear level—whatever the ostensible diplomatic uses of talk about a ' European Nuclear Force ' may be—but is also very significant indeed at the conventional level. Any modification in the structure of the alliance which appeared drastically to weaken the American commitment would cut the ground from under the existing basis of NATO strategy and seriously inhibit the choice and flexibility of any feasible alternative posture for the Western European allies, especially during the negotiating phases.

It seems probable that the Soviet Union and her allies will continue to feel that they have a more serious security problem in relation to Western Europe than *vis-à-vis* each other, and that therefore, whatever changes the Warsaw Pact may undergo, it will be maintained. In this position, the ability of the Western allies to undertake any substantial dismantling, or to make more than token unilateral force reductions, would in practice be severely limited.

The attitude of the United States towards her European commitments is likely to be determined in part by events outside Europe, but there seem no grounds to suppose that the United States will not go on believing that peace in Europe is an important and even vital national interest which she must be prepared to defend. Because she is now coming to share European assumptions about the low level of any external threat, it also seems virtually certain that she will want to achieve this purpose by some less expensive and less rigid scheme than that to which she is now bound; there may well, therefore, be reductions in the size of her conventional military presence on the Continent. This will, in itself, be a cause for concern to the Western allies, although there seems no reason in logic to suppose that the current level of forces deployed on the ground in Europe is a theoretical ' best level '. In some respects, most notably in the provision of what are called ' tactical ' nuclear weapons, there may well be a superfluity of force. But it seems unlikely either that United States forces would be withdrawn entirely, or that the United States herself would initiate any restructuring of her commitments by replacing the multilateral framework with a series of bilateral treaties, or by forgoing the dominant role in the NATO command structure. There is nevertheless a major opportunity for the European members of NATO to take a lead in discussions with the United States about ways in which the security forces of the alliance can be better co-ordinated, more efficiently serviced, and more effectively deployed. It is not an easy area to sweep clear of preconceptions and the shadows of past practice; nor does the nation-state organization of Western Europe allow such prospective improvements in effectiveness as sheer arithmetical comparison with the United States efforts would imply. Both units spend something like $24 billion on European defence each year, but the unified nature and the scale of the United States effort overall allows for a more effective deployment of force, dollar for dollar. However, the ability of Britain, France, and Germany in particular to handle sophisticated military issues through their national operational staffs in many ways puts them in a position to create a genuine exchange of views with the United States; and it must be a matter for regret that the French have not so far joined in the efforts which Britain and Germany, with the other NATO states, have been making to determine common policy viewpoints.

The second major issue which constrains the Western alliance is the position within Germany, which to the Soviet Union still seems to be a possible threat to the stability of the present pattern in Europe. There seems little doubt that although the Western alliance as a whole is formally committed to the reunification of Germany, the allies, including the United States, would be content to accept a position whereby West Germany chose to deal with the reality of East Germany by making a *de facto* recognition and by endeavouring to establish a new position for Berlin. A modified *Ostpolitik* of this kind which led to prolonged and inconclusive negotiations with the East might be more of a strain for West Germany than for her friends, and it might have the effect of making NATO, and perhaps the EEC as well, a less acceptable and less adequate framework within which West German policy can be developed. The American connection is, in the last resort, more important for West German security than the help which the rest of NATO can give; and 'flexibility in response' is a NATO euphemism for a time-buying strategy which almost certainly involves trading German territory for the longer survival of the alliance. No West German government can be expected to welcome this.

It is in this situation that proposals for developing the existing schemes of Western European co-operation into a more extensively and more overtly political association have a special attraction. Besides offering particular gratification to other individual countries, for example the four applicants who want to join the EEC, these schemes may offer an acceptable avenue to West Germany to polarize her interests within an alliance framework and in a way which stirs no new resentments about the past, which in many ways she has so successfully sloughed off. If they are not developed, or they do not prove attractive, West Germany could conceivably turn more readily to a consideration of what benefits she could gain from neutrality.

K

This might not necessarily imply that she would abandon NATO, but it would mean a sharper antithesis between the military and the political aims of her policy, and it might well cause some Western European countries to review critically their attitudes towards concepts of European unity.

To a very limited extent some of the groundwork necessary to develop schemes for unification is being done within the EEC at the present time, as the discussions about the applications from the Converted Four proceed. Western European unification has a long history and already a large literature; the precise form which it should take is likely to be a matter for debate for a long time yet. Besides offering a frame of reference for West German policy, it also offers a basis for developing a common ground for policy-making, in a political context, for Britain, France, and Germany, and the prospect for establishing common viewpoints about the essential requirements of a European security settlement. Agreement is not going to be reached easily, or overnight; there are a great many practical and even mundane issues to be cleared away first, and a wide range of possible structures to be considered. There are, too, a number of conflicting interests which make the prospects for continued co-operation inherently difficult.

To take one example, it is said that Britain and France are naturally complementary units in a number of advanced techniques and skills, like aero-space. It could also be said that they are natural competitors, because their resources cover a broadly comparable range of aptitudes; and the history of such co-operative ventures they have shared that have lasted long enough to have a history demonstrates that, at least in industrial ventures that have an advanced technological content and a positive political appeal, fruitful co-operation is difficult to harvest. Nevertheless, the attempt has to be made to achieve a basic compatibility of general policies, and it is possible to envisage useful preliminary steps which can be taken relatively quickly; though it would be foolish to accept palliative measures of one type, if it appeared, from longer-term considerations, that something else would meet a developing situation better. Moreover, to consider what sort of Western Europe it will be that has to be made secure seems to be an appropriate first priority; and it would mark a significant development from the flaccid attitude which distinguished the West European allies during much of the 1963–8 period of *détente*. It would give rise to a number of questions about what the nature of the Western European relationship should be to the peripheral NATO members —Greece and Turkey in particular. But on the assumption that the general framework of the Atlantic Alliance as a whole is retained and the connection with the United States remains, there is no ostensible reason why the military aspects of the existing security relationships should not also be kept, at least until it becomes clear what general European arrangements become possible.

In this connection, we should consider what a European Security Conference, of the type suggested successively by the Soviet Union, might achieve. It is clear that the Soviet objective has consistently been partly tactical—since to have your adversary suggest that you should make peace, not war, is always unsettling—and partly because the Soviet Union expects that any general discussion about East–West security can be used to legitimize the *status quo* in Central Europe. The suggestions about the issues which might be discussed have now been widened to include economic and technical co-operation, but only in recent months have they become specific enough for observers to be able to discern what points of common importance are emerging. NATO ministers put forward proposals on balanced mutual force reductions with the Warsaw Pact as early as June 1968, and seemed at that time to be developing principles which might provide a framework for discussion of a European Security Conference: no preconditions for a conference should be laid down, any such conference should be adequately prepared, the United States and Canada should participate as equal partners, practical results must be expected to ensue. All these thoughts were dropped for a time after the invasion of Czechoslovakia, and it was not until May 1970 that NATO again showed its hand in any comprehensive fashion. It was then accepted that the two issues proposed by the Warsaw Pact could be developed as an agenda for a conference —guarantees of European security and renunciation of the use of force, or the threat of force, in relations between European states: and the development of economic, scientific and technical relations leading towards political co-operation. But there were important glosses. The NATO communiqué emphasized the need for progress in the separate, but related, discussions about the situation in Germany and Berlin and about the limitation of nuclear weapons. It also renewed the proposals for balanced force reductions, and raised the question of the establishment of permanent machinery that might prepare, and might also follow up, a conference or a series of conferences.

The Warsaw Pact members responded to all these suggestions after their ministerial meeting in Bucharest in June 1970, and essentially accepted that force reductions and some form of institutional arrangement might be agreed topics. The Pact memorandum still, however, urged that a conference should precede, and not follow from, discussions on specific areas; although the participation of the United States and Canada no longer seems a disputed issue, and even the contentions about prior recognition of East Germany have been softened, it still appears to be the case that several more rounds of diplomatic elucidation will be necessary before substantive discussions about issues can begin.

There are obvious difficulties in preparing for a formal review of the problems which not only precipitated the formation of the two blocs but embody all the differences, of substance and attitude, which still divide them. Many of these differences will continue to exist, whether or not there is a conference, and neither side can be sure whether or what sort of benefit can come from such a gathering. Although there may well be divided counsels in the Warsaw Pact about the prospects, we in the West are understandably more conscious of the dilemma in which NATO finds itself. There is no particular point in playing hard to get, and in granting, the Soviet Union easy propaganda points; on the other hand, there is no special virtue in agreeing to a conference before knowing what is going to be discussed, and in what context the discussions are to be held. But the recent NATO moves show that the alliance is aware of the dangers of doing nothing, of sitting unimaginatively on its defensive hocks and of being—as used to be said of the

Treasury in Whitehall—'like an inverted Mr Micawber, waiting for something to turn down'.

Over and above the suggestion for balanced mutual force reductions which has been on the table for some time, the NATO proposals of May 1970 illustrate the type of thinking which has been going on in both official and non-official circles. West German commentators have made some interesting proposals which range from renunciation-of-force declarations by way of arms-control agreements to a permanent European Security Conference.[19] The British suggested, in NATO, the desirability of establishing a standing committee on East–West relations (shortened euphoniously to SCEWER), as a means of preparing for a security conference, and several governments, including the Rumanian, have now expressed interest in some form or other of permanent institutional machinery. Proposals have even been formulated for the siting and structure of such machinery.[20] Also from across the Atlantic, Brzezinski has suggested[21] that a pattern of open-ended discussions could be envisaged rather on the model of the negotiations which led to the Austrian treaty in 1955, and that by viewing the forces of the two alliances as a peace-keeping capability, a European Security Commission might be set up with defined functions like monitoring troop movements and the periodic inspection of force deployments. From specific schemes like these, other, more general schemes to scale down the existing level of military confrontation might be achieved. Clearly, proposals which involve both sets of allies will have to be simple in conception and in execution, in order to reduce to a minimum the opportunities for confusion; but simplicity will be no guarantee that agreement can easily be reached. Nevertheless there appear to be opportunities to dovetail together existing thoughts and ideas on both sides (even if they began as propaganda suggestions) into a useful working agenda, and even into a basis for progress.

[19] See K. Birrenbach & others, *Aussenpolitik nach der Wahl des 6 Bundestages* (Opladen, 1969): also the text of the so-called Bahr paper, in *The Times*, 2 July 1970 which became the basis for the later agreement between the Soviet Union and West Germany on the renunciation of force.

[20] See T. W. Stanley, *A Conference on European Security?* The Atlantic Council of the United States, 1970.

[21] In *Foreign Affairs*, Jan. 1968.

Progress towards what? The time-scale that will be involved is uncertain; security discussions and thoughts of eventual political unification add up to a massive programme which can only be initiated by a positive and consistent exercise of political will. Their achievement, or the proof that they are failing, will take a long time. But because we are talking about a long time-scale, there is evidently nothing incompatible in endeavouring to build a more cohesive and prosperous Western Europe and, at the same time, trying to develop a wider and more general range of relationships with Eastern Europe. The concept of a unified Europe that might bring the present two halves into some form of defined relationship, rather than a mixing together, has even farther to go before it can become conceptually feasible, and can reasonably be left on one side at this stage. It is not reasonable to ignore the opportunities which may conceivably be opening up to reduce the level of tension in the divided Europe of the past generation to a lower and less crudely antagonistic level.

Suggestions for Further Reading

Birnbaum, Karl E. *Peace in Europe: East–West relations 1966–8 and the proposals for a European settlement.* London, OUP for Harvard Center for International Affairs, 1970. (Contains an up-to-date bibliography.)

Buchan, A., ed. *Europe's futures, Europe's choices.* London, Chatto, 1969.

Calleo, David. *Europe's future.* London, Hodder, 1967.

Camps, Miriam. *European unification in the sixties.* London, OUP for RIIA, 1966.

Gordon, Kermit, ed. *Agenda for the Nation.* Washington, Brookings Inst., 1968.

Hass, E. B. *The uniting of Europe.* Stanford UP, 1968.

Grant, Hugo. *Britain in tomorrow's world.* London, Chatto, 1969.

Kissinger, H. A. *American foreign policy, three essays.* London, Weidenfeld, 1969.

—— ed. *Problems of national strategy.* New York, Praeger, 1965.

Northedge, F. S., ed. *The foreign policies of the powers.* London, Faber, 1968.

Pinder, J. & Roy Price. *Europe after de Gaulle.* London, Penguin, 1969.

Contributors to this volume

Neville Brown is Lecturer in International Politics at the University of Birmingham and was formerly Research Assistant at the Institute for Strategic Studies, London. He is the author of several books on strategic studies and contemporary history, writes regularly on defence questions for the *New Scientist* and other periodicals, and is engaged on writing a book on the world in the 1980s.

Alan James is Reader in International Relations at the London School of Economics and Political Science and was Rockefeller Research Fellow at the Institute of War and Peace Studies, Columbia University, New York, during 1968. He is the author of *The Politics of Peace-Keeping* (1969) and numerous articles on international relations.

Peter Nailor is Professor of Politics at the University of Lancaster and was formerly an assistant secretary in the Ministry of Defence. He has been a regular contributor to seminars and publications of the Institute for Strategic Studies.

Kenneth J. Twitchett is Lecturer in Politics at the University of Aberdeen. His publications include (with Carol Ann Cosgrove) *The New International Actors: the United Nations and the European Economic Community* (1970) and numerous articles on international relations.

INDEX

Acoustic sensing, 56–7
Afro-Asian states, 21–2
Albania, 120
Anti-Ballistic Missiles (ABMS), 51–2, 54, 57–62, 64
Anti-submarine surveillance, 56–7
Arab-Israel conflict, 120; role of super-powers, 24–5; *see also* Six-Day War
Arab League, 43 f., 95
Argentina, 64
Arms race, 49; and economic under-development of, 69 ff.; *see also* Nuclear energy; Soviet Union; United States
Atlantic Alliance, *see* Western Alliance
Atlas missile, 52
Australia, 79
Austria, 12, 20, 120

B-52 bomber, 54
Bahrain, 103–4
Balance of power: varied meanings of, 22; inadequate for investigating collaborative strategies, 23; nature of balancing process, 22; question of equilibrium, 23–5; ideological dis-equilibrium and, 25; stable bi-polar situation, 25–6; global system, 26–8; balance of terror, 28–31; increasing importance of economic balance, 31; contrasted with collective security, 32–3
Balance of terror, 24, 28–31
Ballistic-Missile submarines: US, 55–7; Russian, 55; detection of, 55–7; drawbacks of, 57
Belgium, 8
Berlin, 112, 117, 120, 124
Biological weapons, 55
Border claims, and UN, 93
Brandt, Willy, 117
Brazil, 64
Brezhnev, L. I., 116; Brezhnev doc-trine, 39 ff.
Britain, *see* United Kingdom
Brzezinski, Z., 115, 139
Bulgaria, 120

Caamano, Col., 41
Calcutta, population of, 74–5

Canada, 132, 137 f.
CENTO, 38, 41, 44
Chapultepec, Act of (1945), 40
Chemical warfare, 69
Chile, 79
China, Communist, 11, 15, 25–6, 71 f., 85, 122; effects of military security of, 14; annexes Tibet, 25, 30; a potential super-power, 27; influence in Syria and Tanzania, 27;—in South-east Asia, 27; and nuclear power, 29–30, 35, 48, 59 f., 62; and NPT, 64; uranium ' enrichment ', 65; first space satellite, 69; and India, 92; and the UN, 105
Churchill, Winston, suggests a two-tier UN, 42
Claude, Inis, 5, 9, 32
Cobden, R., 18, 130
Cold war, the, 36, 83, 85, 111, 118
Collective-defence and regional arrangements, 38–9; in accord with UN Charter?, 39; the super-powers and alliance policies, 41–2; settle-ment of intra-regional disputes, 42–3; lack of ' security-community ' characteristics, 43–4; *see also* Inter-American system; NATO; SEATO; Warsaw Pact
Collective security: historical and intellectual origins, 31–2; definition of, 32; contrasted with balance of power, 32–3; neither League nor UN conforms to ideal, 33–5; obstacles to practice of, 35–6
Concert of Europe, 32
Congo, 92, 96 f., 100
Conservative Party, 104; Bow Group on W. European nuclear deterrent, 31
Core values: relationship of security with, 4; security as a core value, 8; relative and subjective, 9; and survival of the state, 9–11, 15
Cuba, 10, 25 f., 41, 85, 115
Cyprus, 96–8, 100–2, 106, 120
Czechoslovakia: Soviet invasion of, 7, 12, 89, 91, 118–19, 125, 128, 137; German invasion of, 12; 1948 coup, 112